LIVE IN GRATITUDE DAILY

ISBN-13: 978-1541091313

ISBN-10: 1541091310

Published By ICK com. llc Publishing House©
Edited By ICK Publishing & Denise Joy Thompson

Cover Design By ICK Publishing©

DEDICATION

In dedication to my family. My parents, Roger (Last Alarm May 26, 2015) and Bonnie Thompson, my brother, Kevin, his wife, Julie, and Mandy (and Steve), Ashley, Sadie, Steven, Laney, Emery and Myra. (Jeff not pictured).
As long as we have family, we have abundance, joy, and love.

"Gratitude grows like a field of wildflowers; as the winds carry their seeds to grow and flourish, so do our spoken words of gratefulness grow in the hearts and minds of others."

~ Denise Joy Thompson

CONTENTS

"It is our mindset which determines our success, our mindset which determines "do we go for it"; it is our mindset which creates and receives abundance, joy, and love."

~ Denise Joy Thompson

"Our gratitude determines our attitude; our attitude determines our altitude; how high do you want to go?"
~ Denise Joy Thompson

WELCOME TO YOUR
LIVE IN GRATITUDE DAILY JOURNAL

This 365-day journal is for you to create the life you want. Research shows Gratitude is the foundation for creating and receiving everything we want. Gratitude will not bring you the coveted job or clients if you sit in your house and do not share your gratitude and grow your gratitude every day. Gratitude will bring us what we want as we work (and play) for what we want. Gratitude for a job interview can land you the job, Gratitude to submit a proposal for a contract could get you the contract, Gratitude for a cup of coffee and a conversation could get a Yes when asking for a date. With Gratitude, even if we do not receive what we were looking for at the moment, it does not mean something better will not come along!! Be grateful for every moment, and grateful for every opportunity.

Even though this journal is dated (not year specific), it does not matter on what day you start, you start and then continue for 365 days. Mark the date you start and see what happens when 365 days later you see your first entry. There are prompts and questions for you to think about; this is your journal, and you choose what is helpful to you. You will see how far you have come in Gratitude. I am excited to be doing this along with you!! This is a journey for me also. I will be journaling personally and in the FB group, Live In Gratitude Daily. Join us there for conversations and celebration of our Gratitude's and the changes we see and experience and the changes in those around us. We cannot become more grateful in a vacuum. There will be a ripple effect on those around us; Gratitude is contagious!! It is like a smile, it is like laughter, it will grow, and those around you will benefit as well as you.

This journal is part of my mission of encouraging and supporting everyone to live more loving and fulfilled lives; Gratitude is the KEY (yes, along with healthy eating and exercise). Gratitude will help us to do the tasks we don't want to do; Gratitude will make everything we do seem better--cleaning, cooking, playing, writing, driving, whatever it is. Try it out, Live In Gratitude Daily and see what it does for you. Daily create the Gratitude habit, not the "Grinch" habit or the "Ebenezer Scrooge" habit, create a Live In Gratitude Daily habit. Join us on FB and share, see how it works for others and how it can work for you!! Here is to your Gratitude, the KEY to abundance, joy, and love.

With Gratitude,

Denise Joy Thompson

"Living in gratitude means we are grateful for the important and "unimportant" moments in our life."
~ Denise Joy Thompson

FOREWORD BY

*"It can shift a common day into one of sheer passion,
turn the ordinary into the extraordinary, and
transform times of heartbreak into blessings.
There's no doubt about it. GRATITUDE is a sacred energy.
And, when we look closely, we can find it in the
most obscure and surprising places."*

— *Marsh Engle*

Some many years ago I was invited to speak on the topic of gratitude. Little did I know the words I prepared for the talk would serve as a foundation of strength for all that was destined to unfold – that in a few short months I would enter into a vigorous personal 'initiation' taking the shape of great loss and health crisis stretching me to my very limits. Nor did I know that I would be thrust into a multi-year healing journey requiring I forge a partnership with gratitude, a philosophy I held so close to my heart. This journey would compel me to trust. It would move me to imagine new answers. And, even more importantly, it would motivate me along the most challenging of paths that in the end would affirm to me the life-changing truth that *gratitude is indeed a sacred energy of transformation.*

Without a doubt, times of crisis push us to deepen our relationship with gratitude. Serious illness. The sudden death of someone we love. Business failures. Job loss. Divorce. Heartbreak. It is times like these that test us to our core and can leave us struggling to find any semblance of gratitude. Yet we are compelled to search for it. We search in the darkness. We search in our fears. We reach for it in the seemingly impossible. And, with persistence we somehow find it. We find the richness of gratitude in the very life experiences that appear to be void of gratitude. It's in times such as these that we are gifted the greatest opportunity to allow gratitude into our hearts and infuse our lives with love.

Maybe it is time to look at the state of gratitude from a new vantage point? What if instead of waiting for a crisis to test our strength of gratitude, we create a strong and powerful gratitude mindset now – a point of view that moves us in the direction of seeing, feeling, acknowledging and celebrating moments of gratitude throughout each and every day?

What I know about the sacred energies of gratitude is this:

GRATITUDE is a SUPER POWER.

The world is filled with opportunities to set free the power of gratitude. By stilling our focus, we can find a myriad of magical ways simply waiting for our senses to sharpen to the miracles. And, when that happens, it moves us. It can shift the lens through which we see ANY experience. It can catalyze our actions. It can send us sprinting in the direction of our purpose. It can enlighten. It inspires. And, it can most definitely transform.

Calling upon the words of psychologist William James:

> **"Human beings have the remarkable ability to CHANGE**
> **the way we PERCEIVE things."**

Yes, it's true. As we shift our perspective so do we shift our response. We can naturally become PROACTIVE instead of REACTIVE. By creating a daily practice of gratitude we easily anchor the sacred energies of gratitude into one that becomes our natural state. We can let the super power of gratitude take over our life, have its way with our attitude laying the foundation to live more fully. Through a state of gratitude, we gain the necessary momentum to achieve greater happiness and higher success.

How do we begin to shift into a gratitude mindset?

The easiest and best first step is to align our self with affirmative words and statements that will enliven our perspective and point our sights in the direction of gratitude.

We can begin with *The Five Essential Affirmations of Gratitude* designed to create the environment for gratitude to take root. Then, we can immerse our self in daily practice. Absorbing the words, you will find on the pages of this book is the perfect place to start. This is where gratitude can begin to flourish, each and every moment, each and every day, forever throughout your life.

The First Essential: Gratitude for the Power to Let Go

"Today I let go of the way I think things should be and open to the empowered possibilities of all that can be."

The Second Essential: Gratitude for the Power to Imagine

"Today I remember I AM never too big to ask questions. I never know too much to learn something new, creative and inspired."

The Third Essential: Gratitude for the Power of Faith

"Today I give thanks in advance even before my creative dreams and ideas begin to reveal."

The Fourth Essential: Gratitude for the Power to Lift Another's Spirit

"Today I remember that as I bring joy to the life of another, so do I uplift and inspire my own."

The Fifth Essential: Gratitude for the Power of Serenity

"Today I commit to the awareness I AM always doing the very best I can."

The fact is each of us has a unique path to walk. I know you know this just as I do. Perhaps what we are now inspired to remember is that as we begin to find sheer gratitude for the shifts and changes along the way, we are empowered to live the fullness of our sacred callings. As we honor every step of the journey, we find an exceptional power in all we stand for – and, when we open our hearts to embrace gratitude for it all, we find the freedom to quietly dedicate our life to love.

So, let's do this. Let's allow gratitude in. Let's speak the affirmative words that will liberate us in the sheer power to move mountains, create miracles. Let's agree to create an inspired mark in the world.

Marsh Engle, Founder of The One Million Called
Author of The Sacred Agreements; Dear Amazing Daughter and the acclaimed AMAZING WOMAN multi-book series.

Though best known as a highly inspired motivational speaker and creative consultant to entrepreneurs worldwide, Marsh Engle is also a respected marketing advisor to small business leaders and start-ups. She consults with major corporations and media studios on women's brand initiatives.

As CEO of Marsh Engle Media, a diversified media, career development, publishing and merchandising company, Marsh devotes her passion to creating meaningful campaigns designed to generate worldwide impact. Since 2001 her groundbreaking programs, special events, and speaking engagements have been instrumental in launching the leadership of thousands of women worldwide.

In 2016 she served as a delegate at the UNITED STATE OF WOMEN, an acclaimed leadership program sanctioned by THE WHITE HOUSE. She's been awarded a United States Congressional Proclamation for the establishment of AMAZING WOMAN'S DAY; is a multi-published author; and founder of THE ONE MILLION CALLED, a global movement igniting a NEW WAVE of leadership among women dedicated to building successful projects and brands positioned to benefit millions!

As a single mother, she raised two sons. To this day Marsh believes this to be her most valued accomplishment.

For more information about Marsh Engle and her work, visit www.MarshEngle.com and www.OneMillionCalled.com.

"We must first be grateful for our self before we can be truly grateful
for someone else. Thank "you" today for all
you have done, are doing and will do."
~ *Denise Joy Thompson*

January

*"How wonderful it is that nobody need wait
a single moment before starting
to improve the world."*
~ *Anne Frank*

January 1

The beginning of a New Year; often we wait for the new year to become a "new me". One of the greatest gifts we have is each day an opportunity for a "new me". Each day allows us to move forward, not letting anything from yesterday hold us back. Each day allows us to create the minutes, hours and days we want to live. Each day allows us to count our blessings, even if it is a fact we woke up!! Each day allows us to be grateful for what we have, no matter how small or how large. I was blessed to see Dr. Joe Vitale in December 2013. During his presentation, he recounted one of his greatest gratitude's was what led him to become one of the most prolific teachers and writers of the Law of Attraction. Dr. Joe Vitale, once homeless, became grateful for a pencil. Yes, a pencil.

You have the opportunity to change your life now. With a pencil or pen to write your GRATITUDES each day. Every day fill your heart, mind, and soul with gratitude for what you have. Gratitude is the KEY to abundance, joy, and love.

Denise Joy Thompson is a Wife, Mother of 3 furbabies, a #1 International Best-Seller Author, Coach, Colonel in the Air Force Reserve, a Therapist, and Veteran. She is the host of The Power Of A Woman's Voice TV. Denise's mission is for everyone to have the life they can create. Connect at www.facebook.com/groups/LiveInGratitudeDaily.

_____

_____

_____

_____

_____

_____

_____

_____

_____

 **January 2**

Happy New Year Beautiful!
Let us ring in this New Year, with New Beginnings,
and be grateful for a new second, a new minute, a new hour, a new day,
a new month, a New Quarter, a New Year, to discover who you are.
Step into your Sparkle and Ring in your Beautiful! XOXO

Irene Pro is CEO of ICK Communication llc, which includes ICK Publishing, We Are Beautiful Magazine©, and We Are Beautiful Teens Magazine© Irene lives in New Jersey with her husband, three beautiful children, three dogs, three cats and four chickens!! Connect with Irene at www.wearebeautifulmagazine.community *or* www.facebook.com/wearebeautifulmagazine.

_____

_____

_____

_____

_____

_____

_____

_____

_____

_____

_____

January 3

I Dedicate My Inspirational Message of Gratitude to My Family and Friends

One Life to Live. **Living Life on Purpose**, and being my **Ultimate Self** is the **Desire**, **Hope**, and **Dream**. Every journey and encounter is a path and guide that is leading me to my destiny. Good, bad, or indifferent, the path is a learning experience and a test to prepare me for greatness and my life's purpose. However, I did not always know my destination and how to get there. See, we stay so busy that we don't have time to learn about ourselves and purpose in life. So we are drifting and existing.

I am thankful that I found my purpose in helping people determine their purpose in life. I am also grateful for family and friends who did not judge me as I took risks to explore every option to get me to the next level. I found that if you stay determined, persistent, and focused on whatever you want to accomplish the possibilities are limitless. However, I cannot fail to mention "Sacrifice." The key is to stay **On Course**, **No Matter What**. **Life is Full of Lessons**, **Embrace the Inevitable**, **Live the Life of Abundance** and **Prosperity**.

Dr. Joyce A. Parks is a Business Professor, Entrepreneur, and Leadership Strategist. Joyce has an earned a doctorate in Global Leadership, specializing in Organizational Management, an MBA, and an undergraduate degree in Organizational Leadership and Supervision. Follow Joyce on Twitter at @DrJ_4Leadership.

_____

_____

_____

_____

_____

_____

_____

_____

_____

_____

January 4

Gratitude Grows Happiness

Life is like a garden. If it is well tended, it can be beautiful and rewarding. If it is left to neglect, it becomes unruly, overwhelming and burdensome. One of the keys to becoming a Master Gardener is to plant 'Seeds of Gratitude' on a daily basis. As you mindfully plant your seeds, you create a space of higher positive vibrations, a space of love, a space in which abundance is welcome and lives almost effortlessly. Know that each seed of gratitude holds within it endless life force. Know that each seed holds within it the secret keys to happiness. As you focus on each seed of gratitude, recognizing its gifts, it, in turn, will flourish, thus sustaining and supporting you in every area of your existence.

Laurie Hartley Moore is an Entrepreneur by heart with 30 years of experience. Laurie loves people. She loves creating opportunities that help people acquire their dreams and loves teaching people how to have joy in every aspect of their life. Connect with Laurie at www.ADestinyByDesign.com.

January 5

To My Spirit Sister, Percussion Goddess Crystal Taliefero

What is the message you convey to the world on a daily basis? It is important that we align our hearts with how we live our lives. Every word, every action is observed by our children, other people around us and by those we love and who love us. The gratitude we experience, and we express, creates our life and has a positive effect on those around us.

Be consistent in your delivery, open your heart and allow your love and light to shine in this world. Together we come together to raise the global consciousness and bring light to our shadow side. Once we unite in this cause, darkness can no longer loom in the corners, and we will reside together in our natural state of Peace and Love.

Laura Goodman *The Shameless Warrior(tm) is the embodiment of reverent authentic love. Her mission is to lend her voice to Warriors of abuse who have not found theirs. Laura is an Author, Mentor, Warrior, Teacher, Speaker, and Advocate. She is here to serve humanity and loves with an open heart, fully and completely. Connect with Laura at www.facebook.com/pg/shamelesswarrior.*

January 6

The journey of gratitude from emptiness to abundance is very fulfilling. I never had an idea of gratitude. I am so used to complaining that when I sat down and thought of gratitude for what I have in my life, suddenly I felt so relieved and satisfied. In those moments I felt I already had all the things I asked for and a few things I didn't even ask for. Is life all about perspective, all about the way you see things and take things? This is a whole new concept for me, and it will help me feel happy at any moment of life. Paying gratitude to myself and what I have in life, is one of the strongest choices to overshadow your problems and count your blessings. This choice is totally worth taking as it can change the whole outlook towards life and can guarantee happiness at any point of life. This simple gesture is life changing.

Mansi Parmar was born and raised in India and settled in Canada. Mansi is a Biotechnologist, a Home Maker, and a Crafter. Connect with Mansi at Mansiparmar06@gmail.com.

January 7

In Dedication to My Mom (Kathy Bennett)

What is swirling around in your heart today? Do you give and accept yourself with the same love and to the same degree that you accept and give to everyone else? For many it is much easier to love and give in excess to others then it is to receive from others or even ourselves.

Today's focus is to visit the center of your heart and unlock deep self-love that overflows through you and around you.

Practice this visualization: Stand with your feet on the ground, spine tall and straight. Visualize milky white light pouring into your heart, filling your entire being with the essence of love, grace, and gratitude, to the point of overflow. See the overflow spilling out and pooling around you. The overflow is wholeness, deep self-love and nourishment. Your heart is fully open, and it weaves a thread of love and compassion that ripples out beyond your knowing, creating a profound impact on all those around you, take note of the abundant evidence that is returned to you.

__Dixie Bennett__ is on a mission to educate and empower 1 Million women who are healers and leaders to overcome pain and emotional blocks, so they are freed to make their impact in the world and create joyful abundance while transforming lives. Connect with Dixie at www.stillpointbodyworks.ca.

January 8

"The word gratitude is derived from the Latin word gratia, which means grace, graciousness, or gratefulness (depending on the context). In some ways gratitude encompasses all of these meanings. Gratitude is a thankful appreciation for what an individual receives, whether tangible or intangible. With gratitude, people acknowledge the goodness in their lives. In the process, people usually recognize that the source of that goodness lies at least partially outside themselves. As a result, gratitude also helps people connect to something larger than themselves as individuals — whether to other people, nature, or a higher power."

~ Harvard Health Publications, November 2011
Harvard Medical School

When you think about gratitude or being thankful, what or who do you feel connected to?

_____

_____

_____

_____

_____

_____

_____

_____

_____

_____

_____

January 9

"In positive psychology research, gratitude is strongly and consistently associated with greater happiness. Gratitude helps people feel more positive emotions, relish good experiences, improve their health, deal with adversity, and build strong relationships.

People feel and express gratitude in multiple ways. They can apply it to the past (retrieving positive memories and being thankful for elements of childhood or past blessings), the present (not taking good fortune for granted as it comes), and the future (maintaining a hopeful and optimistic attitude). Regardless of the inherent or current level of someone's gratitude, it's a quality that individuals can successfully cultivate further."

~ Harvard Health Publications, November 2011
Harvard Medical School

When you express gratitude, what is the feeling or emotion you feel?

_____

_____

_____

_____

_____

_____

_____

_____

_____

January 10

In Dedication to Michael

Begin each day with a grateful heart, sometimes you read something somewhere, and it just sticks with you. For me, it is so important to take the first moments of every day and focus on all of the blessings I have in my life. Before my feet hit the ground, I lay in silence and take the time to set my intentions for the day, pray over my life and my loved ones and express gratitude. Depending on my circumstances this may be an expression of thankfulness for another day on this planet or remembering how lucky we are to be free and live in this beautiful country. I try to remember to take time and be grateful for the negative experiences in my life as well and to understand how they have shaped me to be a stronger person. Starting my day this way helps me to stay in a constructive frame of mind and reminds me to be a blessing to others.

Jennifer Eskina is a Financial Professional and a Business Owner in Austin, TX. She feels inspired to lead and help people become financially independent so they can live blessed lives and pour into the lives of other people. Connect with Jennifer at jennifer@thetrustedsolution.com or linkedin.com/jennifereskina.

January 11

"The single greatest thing you can do to change your life today would be to start being grateful for what you have right now. And the more grateful you are, the more you get.
The more you praise and celebrate your life, the more there is in life to celebrate.

Be thankful for what you have; you'll end up having more. If you concentrate on what you don't have, you will never, ever have enough."

-- Oprah Winfrey

What can YOU celebrate today? What went "right" today?

_____

_____

_____

_____

_____

_____

_____

_____

_____

_____

_____

_____

_____

January 12

"Two psychologists, Dr. Robert A. Emmons of the University of California, Davis, and Dr. Michael E. McCullough of the University of Miami, have done much of the research on gratitude. In one study, they asked all participants to write a few sentences each week, focusing on particular topics.

One group wrote about things they were grateful for that had occurred during the week. A second group wrote about daily irritations or things that had displeased them, and the third wrote about events that had affected them (with no emphasis on them being positive or negative). After ten weeks, those who wrote about gratitude were more optimistic and felt better about their lives. Surprisingly, they also exercised more and had fewer visits to physicians than those who focused on sources of aggravation."

~ Harvard Health Publications, November 2011
Harvard Medical School

How is writing about gratitude, focusing on being thankful, increasing positive experiences in your life?

_____

_____

_____

_____

_____

_____

_____

_____

_____

January 13

Would you like to create more abundance in your life this year? ***Express gratitude for every penny flowing in.*** One of the lessons I have learned as a successful business owner is to pay attention to my numbers. This hasn't always been easy. I am super creative, and in the past, I struggled with my relationship with money. Learning to love my numbers started with expressing gratitude for every penny flowing in.

This gratitude practice allowed me to shift my energy and to manifest hundreds of thousands of dollars into my business. I encourage you to pay attention to every penny that you find on the street, the dollar in the dryer, the twenty-dollar bill in a coat pocket, the unexpected refund check, and the income you are earning. The secret to manifesting more money and more freedom in your life is to pay attention and express gratitude for all the abundance already flowing in. Gather your courage and your gratitude and celebrate each and every cent that flows in.

Minette Riordan, Ph.D. *is an award-winning Entrepreneur, Best-selling Author, Wife, Mom, Artist, and Foodie. Ready to manifest more money in your business and have fun doing it? Download Minette's gift of Money, Meditation & Mandalas at* *www.PathtoProfitAcademy.com/mmm*

_____

_____

_____

_____

_____

_____

_____

_____

_____

_____

January 14

A Spirit of Giving

To give is to strengthen the spirit within
For the one who gives away the coat off their back
Will be warmed by the resilience of their heart
And the one who gives their money to those less fortunate
Will be rich in everlasting love

To give is to have the hands of an angel
For the lives you touch become blessed
Sorrow and worry leave their hearts
And they are replaced with hope and gratitude

Sarah Childs *is the Owner of Childs' Play: Games & Geekery. Connect with Sarah at Childsplaygames.com*

_____

_____

_____

_____

_____

_____

_____

_____

_____

_____

January 15

In Dedication to My Daughter

Today, I am blessed with the birth of my daughter and truly thank the Lord for her. There have been some challenging times, however, am appreciative of the Mother/Daughter bond that we share. Grateful to have the opportunity to witness her strong foundation of faith, and knowledge that she knows where to draw her strength when faced with adversity. We each have our moments. However, each time we are challenged, we are able to share in the journey through prayer, tears, sometimes tears of joy, laughter, late night and early morning talks, runs, and exercise. We have done lots of cooking, baking, listening to music, taken adventures, gone for ice cream and just listen to each other and discussing options to achieve the best possible solution for the task at hand. Where there is a will, there is a way. We may just need to be a bit creative and patient. She is an absolute blessing, and am grateful to have her as my daughter and my friend. What life experience are you grateful for?

DeLyla Haunschild is a Mother to two and a College Graduate. DeLyla's faith is the one constant that remains throughout her life; she knows she has so many blessings to be grateful and thankful to the Lord for experiencing. Follow DeLyla at www.facebook.com/DeLylaHaunschild or email at DeLyla.Global.247@gmail.com.

January 16

In Dedication to My Brother, Kevin

Family members often are not chosen; choosing to love who is family is a choice. Through all of the years, there is one constant; we are still family. As I reflect on this day, your birthday, I see how diverse our paths are; not good or bad, not better or worse, but different. My path was to wander, to see far horizons, to help others to grow and find their way. Your path was to have a family, build a home. God did not choose for my path to include children. God's path for you resulted in those gifts; gifts which I will forever cherish. You gave me the gifts of your children and grandchildren.

For these most precious gifts, I am forever grateful.

Denise Joy Thompson is a Wife, Mother of three furbabies, a #1 International Best-Selling Author, Coach, Colonel in the Air Force Reserve, a Therapist, and a Veteran. She is the host of The Power Of A Woman's Voice TV show. Denise's mission is to help all women have a "Voice". Connect at www.facebook.com/groups/liveingratitudedaily and thecoachalliance@gmail.com.

January 17

Here are some ways to cultivate gratitude on a regular basis:

1. Write a thank-you note. You can make yourself happier and nurture your relationship with another person by writing a thank-you letter expressing your enjoyment and appreciation of that person's impact on your life. Send it, or better yet, deliver and read it in person if possible. Make a habit of sending at least one gratitude letter a month.

2. Thank someone mentally. It may help just to think about someone who has done something nice for you and mentally thank the individual.

*3. Keep a gratitude journal. (*Continue to write in **Live In Gratitude Daily**.)

4. Write about your blessings, reflecting on what went right or what you are grateful for. Sometimes it helps to pick a number, such as three to five things, that you will identify each week. As you write, be specific and think about the sensations you felt when something good happened to you.

5. Pray. People who are religious can use prayer to cultivate gratitude.

6. Meditate. Mindfulness meditation involves focusing on the present moment without judgment.

~ Harvard Health Publications, November 2011
Harvard Medical School

January 18

New Beginnings: The definition of gratitude according to the Merriam-Webster Dictionary is the state of being grateful; thankfulness. For me, Gratitude is a state of being that I choose each day to develop as a part of my unique being. There is an inner believe that I am gifted with the breath of life each day, and my God of creation can give and take away in His time. This leaves me in a state of thankfulness that I can have any moment each day to be a difference in this life journey. I start my day with prayers of thanks and counting blessings: I thank my God each day for the gift of the breath of life each moment, for all the blessings I receive. Yes, even the Challenges of I face. All I can say is that He will guide me through and I will be open to following His guidance, through the wisdom and resource I receive, develop a vision, and life direction. My gratitude is for all life has brought me so far.

Martha Chua is a transplant to Mississippi from Singapore. Life journey towards light is her life pursuit of purpose, wisdom, and enlightenment to inspire others with her unique life lessons learned and experienced and to be a difference in lives of others. Connect with Martha at lifejourneytowardslight@gmail.com.

January 19

There's an old saying "if you've forgotten the language of gratitude, you'll never be on speaking terms with happiness." ~ Author unknown.

Research shows gratitude can support in decreasing depressive symptoms. Several studies have shown depression to be inversely correlated to gratitude. It seems that the more grateful a person is, the less depressed they are. Philip Watkins, a clinical psychologist at Eastern Washington University, found that clinically depressed individuals showed significantly lower gratitude (nearly 50 percent less) than non-depressed groups (controls). This research supports the idea that our thoughts influence our emotions. This does not mean if you are on anti-depressants, to stop using them, nor if you are going through a significant loss that the emotional pain will go away. This does mean, though, if we do incorporate thoughts of gratitude and thankfulness into our day, it will offset the not so positive thoughts. Instead of only the depressive or thoughts of loss, we will also have gratitude for something in our life; even if it is for the sun, the wind, the fact we do have a new day.

When you have had a difficult time, identify three things for which you are grateful?

_____

_____

_____

_____

_____

_____

_____

_____

_____

_____

January 20

My gratitude comes from my faith in Jesus as Lord and His sacrifice. Years ago, I began comparing my rights as a "Christian Citizen" to my rights as an American Citizen. I asked this question of several people, "What rights do we have in Christ?" I was told, "We don't have rights. We are to follow God's commands and do what the Bible says." As you can imagine, I was perplexed and dissatisfied. Those answers propelled me into research where I found some very powerful information in the Bible on the subject of rights; not the Bill of Rights, but rather, the Bible of Rights.

In chapter 4 of Galatians, Paul writes that we are no longer slaves, but God's children; since we are his children, God has made us His heirs. Heir means right to inherit. I am grateful for the legal right to be an heir to the throne. I have great comfort knowing that I inherit his love and protection. I spend time daily giving thanks for His sacrifice on my behalf.

Sandy Moriarty *is a Wife and Mother of three kids. She has been a Licensed Attorney for over 20 years. As the Author of the book "My Logical Conclusion" and the blog mylogicalconclusion.com, God's Word is Sandy's logical conclusion for strength and empowerment. Women helping women achieve more is her mission.*

January 21

In Dedication to Gatlen Cash

Today is the day our son was born, the day we became parents and the day our family became 3. I had been anxious about delivering this gift from God and tried to control how it would happen. But God and Gatlen had other plans; He wanted me to be grateful through the storms. Very quickly after starting labor, I was suddenly faced with a life-threatening condition that could have ended both of our lives. At that moment, all my husband and I had was God. Laying on the operating table, we recited The Lord's Prayer to a silent room of bustling people. Then the most beautiful squeak finally filled the room. Gatlen was flawless. Surrendering control to Him had glorified His power. This was a lesson in faith in Him, preparing me for the storms that I'd faced. I gained trust in Him to leave a job that was making me miserable and to begin working for WineShop at Home. It gave me the strength to stay home with my sweet boy despite feeling inadequate. Most importantly, I'm grateful for Gatlen Cash, my daily reminder that blind faith will always yield His perfect plans. Happy Birthday, sweet boy. I love you.

Brittany L. Sumner is a Wife to a wonderful husband, Mother to a rambunctious son and Business Owner at www.crazywinelady.com. She has a passion for helping others, serving her church and enjoying a good glass of wine.

January 22

"God bless the broken road that brought me here to you."
Nitty Gritty Dirt Band
"Good judgment comes from experience.
Experience comes from bad judgment."
~Unknown

My mom knew how to find the black cloud behind every silver lining. A burden was lifted from my shoulders when I realized it's okay to see the glass optimistically half full. A second burden was lifted when I acknowledged that (Duh!) everyone makes mistakes. And, the only mistake about making a mistake is not learning from it. I made several colossal poor choices in my youth. There have been two keys to my surviving and learning from my bad judgment: 1) Everyone screws up; 2) We need to forgive ourselves; we need to not make a similar mistake again, and we need to atone for our mistake if it harmed someone.

My past has led me to where I am now. I would change some things if I could; I didn't know then to make a better decision. I know now and am grateful for that wisdom. "God bless the broken road that brought me" to this point. God bless the experience that has humbled me and taught me to be wiser, more thoughtful, and more understanding about the choices of others. I am grateful for what I have encountered along the way.

Margaret Watson Hopkins, *RN, MN is a Trauma Nurse with over 30 years in the trenches including 12 years as a Flight Nurse. She has taught ICISF certified crisis management courses, emphasizing resilience and recovery from traumatic incidents since 1991. Contact Margaret at m.watson911@sbcglobal.net.*

January 23

"Every day, think as you wake up, today I am fortunate to be alive, I have a precious human life, I am not going to waste it. I am going to use all my energies to develop myself, to expand my heart out to others; to achieve enlightenment for the benefit of all beings. I am going to have kind thoughts towards others, I am not going to get angry or think badly about others. I am going to benefit others as much as I can."

~ *Dalai Lama XIV*

Whether you are reading this in the morning or at night, what are you fortunate (grateful) for?

_____

_____

_____

_____

_____

_____

_____

_____

_____

_____

_____

_____

_____

January 24

In Dedication of My Husband

Dear Jerry,

I am grateful for your everlasting love that you had given to the kids and I. Even when we did not have the strength to stand by your side as I hoped we could. You have never complained but rather embraced us with the capabilities that you had, which diminishing day by day. You left us in this world still taking care of us through your preparations before death. I understand now that I will always be taken care off until my death.

Because of this journey, I love deeper than I have ever before. I appreciate life and the gift of it. I value the moments of everyday life. I laugh more. I am developing thankfulness.

Until we see again,

Dani

Daniela Krotzer is a Mom of two precious children who lost our protector and provider to Cancer. At the age of 41, I became a Widow. What defines me is not my loss or suffering, but how I embrace the hope in it, live through it and take steps by faith to conquer it. Contact Daniela at danielakrotzer@gmail.com.

January 25

The journey to gratitude is not always an easy one. In a world full of one-click purchases, instant gratification, and access to all information imaginable, our gratitude can be lost in a cloud of invisible complacency. Gratitude is an important trait with great perks: outcomes include better sleep, additional compassion, and stronger immune systems. How do we take the search for gratitude to a new level? My method is subtraction.

My subtraction began in the happenstance stumbling years of early adulthood where I dealt with many a loss and constant sacrifice in pursuit of my career and moving forward. I realize now I am a better person for having gone without for so long, and I hold more appreciation for the small comforts of home. I still rely on subtraction to keep focus. Two years ago, I traded sleeping in for marathon training; recently it was coffee. Now I am so much more grateful for the peaceful simplicity of sleeping in and having a homemade latte on a Sunday morning, after a week of hard work.

Mary Scheske Wharmby *is a Business Owner helping small businesses and non-profits market themselves successfully. She is an Alumnae of Texas A&M University and resides in New Braunfels, Texas where she manages a small business and home.*
Contact Mary at _mary@marymakingtx.com_ *or* _http://facebook.com/marymakingtx._

January 26

"The ship of my life may or may not be sailing on calm and amiable seas. The challenging days of my existence may or may not be bright and promising. Stormy or sunny days, glorious or lonely nights, I maintain an attitude of gratitude. If I insist on being pessimistic, there is always tomorrow. Today I am blessed. "

~ Maya Angelou

Gratitude does not mean one will not have trials and tribulations. Living in "gratitude" means we do not veer far off course when problems do arise since we are able to "course correct" and remember what we have in our life.

What are one or two things in your life you can be grateful for if even going through a difficult time?

_____

_____

_____

_____

_____

_____

_____

_____

_____

_____

_____

_____

January 27

Dedicated to My Mother and Father who Taught Me to find style & beauty in vintage pieces.

"When you don't dress like everyone else, you don't have to think like everyone else." - Iris Apfel. When I was in elementary school, my family didn't have a budget for name brand clothes. My mom taught herself to sew in high school and would often make my clothes, or my dad would bring home pieces for me that he found at yard sales. A handmade vest and vintage cashmere sweater- what more could a girl ask for? Even though it wasn't trendy back then, I learned at a young age that style comes from within. It's about finding pieces that you love, from people that you love, that make you feel FABulous inside.

I am so happy and grateful for my favorite piece of clothing: _____. When I wear it, I feel _____.

Allison "FAB" Howell- Social Worker by day, Life Stylist by night teaching women to feel FABulous in Life & Style. Allison combines experience in fashion and psychology to inspire lives to be fun, fresh, and full of FABulous love. www.FABover.com.

_____

_____

_____

_____

_____

_____

_____

_____

_____

_____

_____

_____

_____

_____

January 28

"I have lived large parts of my life in wonderful circumstances that I utterly failed to appreciate. Reasons to be happy were everywhere, but somehow I didn't connect with them. It was as though I was eating but couldn't taste the food. Finally, I've learned to celebrate the good while it's happening. I feel gratitude and praise today for what are sometimes such simple pleasures. I have learned that happiness is not determined by circumstances. Happiness is not what happens when everything goes the way you think it should go; happiness is what happens when you decide to be happy."

~ Marianne Williamson

What can you celebrate today, right now? List three things, big or small to celebrate and be grateful for!

_____

_____

_____

_____

_____

_____

_____

_____

_____

_____

_____

January 29

*"Have you ever tried to pay someone a compliment and seen them embarrassed, confused, or even somewhat irked at your offering of kindness, love, and admiration? Or maybe, you have been on the receiving end and found yourself uncomfortable and unable to respond with gratitude and grace. This everyday example of the difficulties that can arise when we are offered a gift reveals one of the important principles of learning how to receive the abundance that the Universe holds for us. In order to manifest, to take part in the process of co-creating your life and attracting to yourself the objects of your heart's desires, **you must know that you are worthy of receiving**. Manifesting involves using the power of your inner world to craft a fuller relationship with life. You can remind yourself all day long that the same power that brought anything into the physical world also brought you, but if you do not feel worthy, you will disrupt the natural flow of energy into your life and create a blockage that makes manifestation impossible. **Remember that you are worthy of abundance. Feeling worthy of any blessings or desires is a feature of your inner life.**"*

~ Dr. Wayne Dyer

List all of your "abundance" and receive; be grateful for all you have.

_____

_____

_____

_____

_____

_____

_____

_____

_____

_____

January 30

In Dedication of My Son

Today, I am grateful for being blessed with a son, and the world of parenthood. It is amazing how this miracle of life can be ever so life changing. It is extraordinary how this life can make such an impact in our world. It has been a long journey and continues to keep the faith through this mother/son relationship. Even though we have had our moments, I am truly thankful to the Lord for him. What life changing event are you grateful for?

DeLyla Haunschild is a Mother to two and a College Graduate. DeLyla's faith is the one constant that remains throughout her life; she knows she has so many blessings to be grateful and thankful to the Lord for experiencing. Follow DeLyla at www.facebook.com/DeLylaHaunschild or email at DeLyla.Global.247@gmail.com

January 31

Today is January 31st. Where are you in your expectations for 2017 and every year after? Are you already in disappointment and regret? I think at times we treat daily gratitude as a quick fix to feel better about ourselves and our lives. My experience is that we first need to acknowledge what isn't working; what is causing us pain or challenging us; or what is disappointing us. Then **LET IT GO** – hand it over to Your Higher Power/God/The Universe (whoever that is for you).

THEN and **ONLY THEN**, acknowledge what you are grateful for! It will be cleaner, stronger, and more powerful. It will be able to be offered to the heavens – heard clearer & more impactful. That will clear the road for abundance & prosperity. That will make your daily gratitude more intentional & constructive. **REMEMBER:** Acknowledge, Let it Go, Be Grateful!

Brenda B. Bailey *is a Certified Belief Integration Specialist, Coach, and Consultant. Connect with Brenda at www.facebook.com/unlimitedpossibilities101.com and www.UnlimitedPossibilities101.com.*

"We must first be grateful for our self before we can be truly grateful for someone else. Thank "you" today for all you have done, are doing and will do."

~ Denise Joy Thompson

February

February 1

In Memory of My Granduncle, My Guardian and Supporter

How does one remain in a state of gratitude, when life grows challenging? For me, Gratitude is a state of being that I choose each day to develop as a part of my unique being. This is a state that I have been tested, trial and "baptism by fire". For years I have been in caregiving. Many times, it seems like I am alone in a crowd. Undoubtedly, there are many who will be the first to tell you what to do, but when it comes to the being present, one can count on the fingers. He had been the silent presence during the years I cared for my granny. Yet life is such, I had immigrated and was not there when He passed away. How often do you tell your loved ones, I love you, thank you for being in my life. Because someday may never come.

Martha Chua is a transplant to Mississippi from Singapore. Life journey towards light is her life pursuit of purpose, wisdom, and enlightenment to inspire others with her unique life lessons learned and experienced and to be a difference in lives of others. Connect with Martha at lifejourneytowardslight@gmail.com

February 2

1) "Gratitude opens the door to ... the power, the wisdom, the creativity of the universe."

2) "No matter what the situation is ... close your eyes and think of all the things in your life you could be grateful for right now."

3) "Every negative thought weakens the partnership between mind and body."

~ Deepak Chopra

Gratitude begins in our mind, we decide to think about gratitude and be grateful. As we **"Live In Gratitude Daily"** we no longer have to "think" about gratitude, we are gratitude. We become truly aligned and are now living, not "practicing" gratitude.

How do you see Gratitude in yourself and your actions?

_____

_____

_____

_____

_____

_____

_____

_____

_____

_____

_____

_____

_____

_____

February 3

"For me, every hour is grace. And I feel gratitude in my heart each time I can meet someone and look at his or her smile."

~ Elie Wiesel

Gratitude does not make us selfish. True gratitude in you, actually makes you less selfish and more loving towards others. Gratitude is the **KEY** to abundance, joy and **LOVE**.

Who are you to grateful to see smile?

_____

_____

_____

_____

_____

_____

_____

_____

_____

_____

_____

_____

_____

_____

February 4

You cannot move forward until you make peace with where you are at now.

Being grateful for all the good things in life; the simple pleasures and wonders can be a fairly easy and a simple thing to do most of the time. It's finding the deep gratitude within the most challenging and painful times of our lives that requires much more effort on our part and is easy to forget to do but can be the most powerful act that will propel you forward to the next moment. They say hindsight is 20/20 but what if you could have that hindsight now, instead of years later? What if in your darkest moments, your deepest challenges and your greatest emotional pain you could find that place within you where there is gratitude for the experience. I call this place the G- Spot!! That place of Gratitude in the very center of the emotional pain you are feeling. I found mine, and I know you can too … Breath into it, bring the thought, the energy of gratitude into your challenge and allow it to begin to transform you now.

Joy Brugh is a Life Transitions Coach, Shaman and Energy Healer specializing in empowering women through life's challenges and helping them to transform using a unique combination of modern life coaching, energetic and shamanic healing along with crystalline activations. Visit her at www.joybrugh.com or joy@joybrugh.com

February 5

"If the only prayer you said in your whole life was, 'thank you',
it would be enough."
~ Toni Morrison

Sometimes we become so caught up in the business of life; we do not even acknowledge the small courtesies in life. Some have a difficult time accepting gratitude; sometimes we brush aside someone thanking us. We are worthy of giving and receiving thanks. We are worthy of abundance, joy, and love which are the by-products of gratitude.

Accept and give gratitude freely.

What were you thanked for today and what did you thank someone else for?

_____

_____

_____

_____

_____

_____

_____

_____

_____

_____

_____

February 6

"No gesture is too small when it is done with gratitude."

~ Oprah

I appreciate on garbage days my neighbor brings the empty garbage can up to the garage. If he leaves before the garbage is picked up, then I will place his by his garage. I will also pick up his paper if it is the driveway. These are small things to do, it is neighborly and is given and received with gratitude. When we see each other, we acknowledge the "favors" with a wave and a nod.

What are the small things you do for others and are done for you in gratitude? (Did you realize the gratitude was there?)

_____

_____

_____

_____

_____

_____

_____

_____

_____

_____

_____

February 7

"Gratitude unlocks the fullness of life. It turns what we have into enough, and more. It turns denial into acceptance, chaos to order, confusion to clarity."

~ Melody Beattie

When we are overwhelmed, often looking at what we have is not on our mind. If when we are overwhelmed, we take a moment to "take stock" of what we have, the change in our emotion and energy will probably allow us to think more clearly and figure out what our next step is in regards to decreasing our "overwhelm".

What or whom do you have in your life that you are grateful for and is often the thing/person you go to when you are overwhelmed?

_____

_____

_____

_____

_____

_____

_____

_____

_____

_____

_____

_____

February 8

There are three stages of gratitude, each one more effective than the one before.

1. Feeling grateful for the good things in your life. (This **Live In Daily Gratitude** journal is helping you to do this.)

2. Expressing your gratitude to the people who have made your life better. When you express gratitude to someone else, an emotional bond is formed, and emotional bonding is one of the key traits of truly happy people

3. Adopting new behavior as a result of interacting with those who have helped you. When your gratitude leads to showing more sympathy, less judgment, and a greater appreciation for life itself, you are setting the stage for years of positive reinforcement.

By adopting gratitude as your default position, so to speak, you tell your brain that positive input is going too far outweigh negative input. Mixed signals lead to mixed results. By being consistent in your attitude of gratitude, you set down a blueprint that over time leads to brain changes with farseeing benefits.

--Excerpts from An Important Thing to Make You Healthier: Gratitude;

~Deepak Chopra

How are you consistently practicing Gratitude? Create your "blueprint of gratitude" by writing your gratitude's every day.

_____

_____

_____

_____

_____

_____

_____

_____

_____

February 9

In Honor of a Father's Love

A Father's love is an absolute gift. It is paramount how a gentleman can have such an impact in one's life by being a role model expressing his kind, caring heart, faith, patience, tough work ethic, and genuine support and trust in the Lord. It is interesting how a true father can step in and become one's family without being blood-related. Thank you for being you and blessing the lives of others.

Who are you grateful for?

DeLyla Haunschild is a Mother to two and a College Graduate. DeLyla's faith is the one constant that remains throughout her life; she knows she has so many blessings to be grateful and thankful to the Lord for experiencing. Follow DeLyla at www.facebook.com/DeLylaHaunschild or email at DeLyla.Global.247@gmail.com.

_____

_____

_____

_____

_____

_____

_____

_____

_____

_____

_____

_____

February 10

"You say grace before meals. All right. But I say grace before the concert and the opera, and grace before the play and pantomime, and grace before I open a book, and grace before sketching, painting, swimming, fencing, boxing, walking, playing, dancing and grace before I dip the pen in the ink."

~ G. K. Chesterton

Do we take the little things for granted? Do we take special occasions for granted? Do we forget to be grateful for all of our experiences? What did you experience today which you are grateful for (even if it was only a cup of coffee)?

_____

_____

_____

_____

_____

_____

_____

_____

_____

_____

_____

_____

_____

February 11

"Gratitude helps you to grow and expand; gratitude brings JOY and laughter into your life and into the lives of all those around you."

~ Eileen Caddy

Have you ever been thankful and in a bad mood? I do not think it can be done. Go ahead, be thankful right now, choose something and be thankful, what is the feeling? Is it happy, joy, contentment, are you smiling, laughing, there are no negative feelings right? Not one; now you might be thinking this is silly, it worked though right, you were not grateful and angry at the same time.

What can you be grateful for right now to change your mood?

_____

_____

_____

_____

_____

_____

_____

_____

_____

_____

_____

_____

February 12

Gratitude has the potential to create a better day, to enhance all your value which is a treasure deep in your soul. Gratitude is spontaneous thankfulness, for yourself and others. The phrase "trade expectations for appreciations" has made my life easier to go through. The more you (I) feel gratitude, the more real it becomes. Your brain will believe it the more and more you practice.

When you go outside do you ever feel thankful for the air you breathe or the body you have (even though it may not be the way you want it to be)? One of the most grateful moments I had was a few years ago, our family was at a kids concert, and the guy was singing the Toy Story song "You got a friend in me" that moment I looked at the kids and felt an indescribable, overwhelming sense of gratitude. These are the moments of gratitude which let us know how precious life is and to treat it well. Every morning you wake up to give thanks for your life, for everything you have in your life at that moment.

Josh Drewien *was born and raised in Seattle Washington. Josh now lives in Idaho with his family, including three children. In 2016, Josh became a Life Coach to help people find meaning in their lives. Contact Josh at jdrewien@gmail.com.*

February 13

Dedicated to My 1st Born, Adrian Pineda. May you bring Love to all in your life as you have brought Love into mine.

One can always start over, no matter where you are on your path in life. I've been at the bottom, with one foot out the door and I'm grateful to myself that I didn't take that last step because today I'm the happiest I've ever been. Self-love is what got me to where I am. I won't tell you it's easy but it is possible and when you see that light at the end of the tunnel, the possibilities become endless! It's all about the choices we make, and I choose LOVE. I give gratitude every day which this is the choice I made!

Here's to second chances!!!

Alma Soul Pineda moved to Maui, Hi from Los Angeles, CA in 2015. She embodies the Aloha spirit. A Mother of two amazing young men, she was drawn to Maui, to inspire and help others see the beauty in life through Love, Faith, and Trust. She also envisions the world being able to heal holistically. Contact Alma at https://thebiomatmiracle.com.

February 14

Gratitude is like magic. Once you truly understand the meaning of gratitude, your life begins to shift in ways that are unimaginable. Your heart becomes so full you can't quite put it into words. It's a feeling that will change your life forever. Now doesn't that sound nice? Remember that every day you have choices. I choose to live by the 3 C's of life. Choices, chances, and changes. You must make a choice to take a chance to change your life. As Tony Robbins would say, "It is in your moments of decision that your destiny is shaped." If you don't like the life surrounding you, remember you are the one who created it, and you have the choice to change it. Such a simple yet complex concept. Even when life throws you a curve ball and you don't know how you will rise above just take a deep breath, get still and remember what you're grateful for; know it's just a bump in the road to teach you a lesson that's for your highest good.

Brianne N. Dodd *is a fun-loving Free Spirit who enjoys helping others find their purpose. As a Reiki Practitioner and Hairstylist Brianne has been given the gift to touch the lives of many. In fact, as a child, she knew her purpose was to lead and help others and so her journey began. Brianne is at beautyandbalancebybrianne@gmail.com.*

February 15

Gratitude in the Face of Adversity

In life some people plan out their entire lives expecting to achieve a certain goal by a certain date, expecting certain people always to be there, and go exactly as they planned. Unfortunately, life can be a bit rocky or even feel like an earthquake shook them upside down. I didn't think this could've happened to me, but it did. My life shook in directions I couldn't understand, but I trusted on the mustard seed of faith I had and trusted in God's plan for my life.

I have a heart full of gratitude for the people who stepped up to help me rebuild. I would even do the same for you just because it's the right thing to do.

Just be grateful, thankful, and appreciate the fact that you aren't fighting your battles alone. You have the strength, determination, and the will of God on your side and he will not fail you. Humble yourself before Him, and He will be kind to you.

Vienna Haunschild is a College Student, Athlete, Business Prodigy, Entrepreneur, 90's kid, Inspirational Leader, Adventure Junkie, Visionary, Philanthropist, Realist, Fashionista, Social Media Consultant, Business Analyst, Future WAG, Common White Girl, Dynamic, Classy, Presidential, Sophisticated, Unconventional, Unique, Wise. Vhaunschild@tlu.edu or @vhaunschild24 on Twitter or @viennah15 on Instagram

February 16

"I am NOT a product of my circumstances; I AM a product of my decisions."

~ Stephen Covey

Decide today to **"Live In Gratitude Daily"**. Think and be grateful and thankful every day, for yourself, your life, others, whatever you have in life, be grateful, acceptance of all you have does not mean you cannot move forward.

Gratitude is the **KEY** to **abundance, joy, and love**. Decide today, decide **NOW**, **DECIDE**.

What can you be grateful for right now, what do you decide to be grateful for?

_____

_____

_____

_____

_____

_____

_____

_____

_____

_____

_____

_____

_____

_____

_____

February 17

"The miracle of gratitude is that it shifts your perception to such an extent that it changes the world you see."

~ Dr. Robert Holden

When we incorporate Gratitude into our daily thinking, it changes our whole perception of what we have and what we need. After two deployments I have a different perspective of what I need. I am more grateful for electricity and running water, hot and cold than I was before. I am more grateful for the quiet, not the days and nights filled with jet engines and other loud noises. It is also nice, not hearing the sirens and alarms of "incoming". I "live in gratitude daily" for returning home.

What do you have in your life today are you grateful for, which in the past you have taken for granted?

_____

_____

_____

_____

_____

_____

_____

_____

_____

_____

_____

_____

February 18

"We think we have to do something to be grateful or something has to be done in order for us to be grateful, when gratitude is a state of being."

~ *Iyanla Vanzant*

The idea of "do unto others" becomes automatic when we practice gratitude. Our gratitude for our self, what we have, what we can do, what we can work for, begins to "rub off" on other people. We begin to fully "practice gratitude" because we have become gratitude in thought, word, and deed. Once we fully are in the "state of gratitude" we cannot help but "live in gratitude daily". Our thoughts, words, and deeds of gratitude are now the "true" us. We have evolved into a "gratitude being".

Think about what has changed about and "in" you since you started journaling. What do you notice?

_____

_____

_____

_____

_____

_____

_____

_____

_____

_____

_____

_____

_____

February 19

"Express your gratitude to the people who have made your life better."

~ Deepak Chopra

How do you let people know you appreciate them? In this world of hurry up, faster is better; we often forget to say "thank you." We might forget to send the email, text, PM or the long forgotten letter to show our gratitude and appreciation.

Think about the last few days, who are you grateful for and why no matter how big or small the reason?

Now let these people know you are grateful, through whatever means available, reach out and see how it feels to be "present in gratitude". How it feels to specifically take a the moment and share your gratitude with them. Share regardless of the outcome or response. Some people do not how to take gratitude and may be embarrassed or brush it off. This is important, for you and them.

_____

_____

_____

_____

_____

_____

_____

_____

_____

_____

_____

February 20

"Acknowledging the good that you already have in your life is the foundation for all abundance."

~ Eckhart Tolle

Gratitude makes us attractive; we create positive energy by being grateful, positive energy attracts more positive energy. If we are grateful for the "abundance" we have, this "abundance gratitude" will allow us to attract and accept more abundance and we will experience joy and love while doing this. We see so many people unhappy yet they have what we think is "abundance". If they do not see it as abundant, then to them it is not, and they are not abundant and they are not happy. It is the mindset of "lack of abundance" (when abundance is there) which creates a prison of unhappiness, not the actual lack of abundance.

What skills and talents do you have which others see as "abundance" which you might discount, or not be grateful for? Often we overlook the very talent others would love to have. Now be grateful for what these skills and talents have done for you?

_____

_____

_____

_____

_____

_____

_____

_____

_____

February 21

> *"The person who grows with a habit grays with it."*

~*North African proverb*

I want to be gray; this means I am living to a ripe old age (it doesn't mean I don't dye it!!) If I practice and live gratitude then it will be with me as I age (and gray).

How are you practicing gratitude? Are you journaling, writing down your thoughts on a daily basis, are you thinking about what you have in your life? Are you appreciating what your family and friends do for you and thanking them for it?

Practice until the "habit" becomes so much a part of you, it is like you always had it.

_____

_____

_____

_____

_____

_____

_____

_____

_____

_____

_____

February 22

In Honor of Grandma Marie

She was only 4'11" but her heart, so full of love and gratitude, touched everyone she met. Grandma Marie was born 2/22/1890 in Russia and came to the US at age four. Growing up in Nebraska, she had to quit school after 3rd grade to work the beet fields. Yet her early hard life never defined Grandma Marie. In her 98 years, she constantly expressed gratitude; for every meal, for her friends and family, for her health and strength to tend her rose garden. I never heard her complain.

I was inspired by her consistency of helping others while maintaining her calm strength through her steadfast faith. She poured a cement walk by herself at 94 and showed it proudly. I believe Grandma Marie's gratitude for daily living shined through everything she did, and everyone she touched.

The way she lived taught me to look outside myself and help those less fortunate. Because of her example, I know the best way to uplift myself and others is turn to gratitude. Expressing gratitude shifts focus from problems to solutions, from heartache to inner calm, from fear to strength.

Cheryl Krieger "CK" Brown is a Musician/Songwriter, Motivational Speaker, and Transformational Trainer. CK's positive music and visioning inspire and uplifts people to their highest and best. CK is grateful to live on a lake in the Pacific Northwest with husband Matthew and four orange kitties. Connect with CK at www.CKBrown.com.

 **February 23**

I am grateful to be alive to leave my sparkle & light everywhere I go…to know I've left my mark of complete happiness.

Alexandria Prokopiw *is a College Student and lives in New Jersey.*

How are you leaving your "sparkle and light"? What are you doing to leave "gratitude" wherever you go?

_____

_____

_____

_____

_____

_____

_____

_____

_____

_____

_____

_____

_____

_____

_____

February 24

"Count your blessings every day,
See them multiply before your eyes.
Gratitude grows wherever it is sown.
Gratitude is limitless and
Shines a light where it is shown."

~Denise Joy Thompson

As you continue to "Live In Gratitude Daily", where can you shine your light of Gratitude? Identify three places to share your Gratitude.

_____

_____

_____

_____

_____

_____

_____

_____

_____

_____

_____

_____

February 25

"I offer my gratitude for the safety and well-being I have been given.

I offer my gratitude for the blessing of this earth I have been given.

I offer my gratitude for the measure of health I have been given.

I offer my gratitude for the family and friends I have been given.

I offer my gratitude for the community I have been given.

I offer my gratitude for the teachings and lessons I have been given.

I offer my gratitude for the life I have been given."

~ Jack Kornfeild

What, or for whom, do you offer your gratitude for?

_____

_____

_____

_____

_____

_____

_____

_____

_____

_____

_____

February 26

"Gratitude is so powerful it decreases judgment of others.
The focus of one's life is of acceptance and support."

~ Denise Joy Thompson

When we truly embrace a **"Live In Gratitude Daily"** life our perspective of everything changes. We become less judgmental of others; we see the value in different perspectives, we live more peacefully, and we accept and support others, despite differences. We are slower to anger; we are slower to give in to frustration and anxiety, we are slower to give up, and we are slower to engage in negative self-talk live. We also will be more positive, more willing to lend a helping hand, and see the glass as "full".

What do you notice is different in how you interact with others, how you view the world and how you view yourself?

_____

_____

_____

_____

_____

_____

_____

_____

_____

_____

_____

_____

February 27

"We think we have to do something to be grateful or something has to be done in order for us to be grateful, when gratitude is a state of being."

~ Iyanla Vanzant

The idea of "do unto others" becomes automatic when we practice gratitude. Our gratitude for our self, what we have, what we can do, what we can work for, begins to "rub off" on other people. We begin to fully "practice gratitude" because we have become "gratitude" in thought, word, and deed. Once we fully are in the "state of gratitude" we cannot help but "live in gratitude daily". Our thoughts, words, and deeds of gratitude are now the "true" us. We have evolved into a "gratitude being".

Think about what has changed about and "in" you since you started journaling. What do you notice?

_____

_____

_____

_____

_____

_____

_____

_____

_____

_____

_____

_____

February 28

To Celebrate My Passage Into This World

When we live in Love and not fear, we see the world in a positive light. Our heart opens and compassion springs forth for all who cross our path. This is the heart meeting itself and light always lead our path forcing our shadows out of hiding. When we live in Love, we also live in gratitude. We live in gratitude for everything in our life, we share and help others to live in gratitude also. If one loves, one is grateful; gratitude cannot exist in hate; gratitude exists in love.

I live in full transparency allowing my life and my heart to be a testament to a life well-lived. I am grateful every day for my journey and where my travels have led me. I am grateful to begin a new day every morning and to live life to the fullest. I lead by example, living a life rich in love, integrity, and vulnerability. I lead by being grateful.

Laura Goodman *The Shameless Warrior(tm) is the embodiment of reverent authentic love. Her mission is to lend her voice to Warriors of abuse who have not found theirs. Laura is an Author, Mentor, Warrior, Teacher, Speaker, Advocate. She is here to serve humanity and loves with an open heart, fully and completely. Connect with Laura at www.facebook.com/pg/shamelesswarrior.*

In recognition of Cheryl Krieger "CK Brown and her songwriting:

GOTTA MOVE ON (TO THE BEST OF ME)   CK Brown and Freebo 2011
VERSE 1:
Yesterday I told the world I thought I was a goner
Reflecting on bad memories became my badge of honor
Tragic tales of all the times I lost my greatest chance
Like Cinderella full of dreams, missed going to the dance.

VERSE 2:
I was paralyzed and prisoned by the darkness of my days
To find the path to happiness I'd better change my ways
The golden key to live my dreams lies in simplicity
Like a child's colored rainbow kite dancing on the breeze.

CHORUS:
No more remembering my sad tale
No more remembering times I failed
No more remembering the Used To Be
Gotta move on to set me free
Gotta move on to The Best of Me.

VERSE 3:
Today I choose to talk about the best side of the story
Shine my holy beacon on the triumph and the glory
Paint a perfect picture of just where I'd like to fly
Focusing the looking glass on diamonds in the sky.

CHORUS:
No more remembering   my sad tale
No more remembering   times I failed
No more remembering   the Used To Be
Gotta move on to set me free
Gotta move on to The Best of Me.

BRIDGE:
The answer you've been searching for is in your attitude
Turn wanting into knowing, regret to gratitude

CHORUS 2X:
No more remembering my sad tale
No more remembering times I failed
No more remembering the Used To Be
Gotta move on to set me free
Gotta move on to The Best of Me.

Gotta move on Gotta move on,
Gotta move on to The Best of Me.

"We need to be in love with each day."

~ Denise Joy Thompson

*"Be thankful for all that others do for you;
be thankful for all you do for yourself."*

~ Denise Joy Thompson

March

March 1

Dedicated to my Sweet Earth Angel, Prema Love

Forgiveness comes in time. We forgive those who have harmed us. This takes the willingness to give up the story or identification of who we are in relation to what happened to us.

Self-forgiveness is the ultimate act of self-love. This comes as a result of giving up holding our self-hostage for anything that causes us suffering or shame.

Once we finally surrender all that we believe ourselves to be, we open our hearts to the authentic love of self that allows us to fall deeper in love with who we are.

Welcome Home Dear One, I have waited a lifetime to meet you!

I am thankful you are here.

Laura Goodman The Shameless Warrior(tm) is the embodiment of reverent authentic love. Her mission is to lend her voice to Warriors of abuse who have not found theirs. Laura is an Author, Mentor, Warrior, Teacher, Speaker, and Advocate. She is here to serve humanity and loves with an open heart, fully and completely. Connect with Laura at www.facebook.com/pg/shamelesswarrior.

_____

_____

_____

_____

_____

_____

_____

_____

_____

_____

_____

March 2

"Gratitude creates a new lens through which we see the positive in every person, situation and experience."

~ Denise Joy Thompson

Often it is easier to see the negative or be dissatisfied with life. When we are living in gratitude, we are more likely to see the positive in everything in our life. Even if we have an experience which is not what we would have liked, we can accept and learn from it, we see our growth by seeking the positive.

Think about the last few days, how have you looked at things differently, using the "lens" of gratitude?

_____

_____

_____

_____

_____

_____

_____

_____

_____

_____

March 3

"The foundation for abundance is to acknowledge and be grateful for what we already have in our life."

~ Denise Joy Thompson

"What we focus on grows." Focusing on what we have, being grateful and appreciative of the people, possessions and money in our life opens "the door" for more abundance. When we have learned to be appreciative of "any" abundance, we are more likely to recognize the opportunity for more abundance. We attract opportunities for abundance and we say "yes" to that abundance.

What abundance do you now recognize you already had before beginning your Live In Gratitude Daily journey? What abundance has come into your life since starting your Live In Gratitude Daily journey?

_____

_____

_____

_____

_____

_____

_____

_____

_____

_____

_____

March 4

In Dedication of My Mother

Today, I truly thank the Lord for the gift of my Mother. She has been instrumental in our lives, teaching us how to persevere even through the toughest of times while keeping the faith. How does one ever thank a person's mother properly for being the strong role model through life's journey? She is an absolute blessing and I am grateful and thankful to the Lord for her.

Who is the person that has made an impact in your life that you are in gratitude of?

DeLyla Haunschild is a Mother to two and a College Graduate. DeLyla's faith is the one constant that remains throughout her life; she knows she has so many blessings to be grateful and thankful to the Lord for experiencing. Follow DeLyla at www.facebook.com/DeLylaHaunschild or email at DeLyla.Global.247@gmail.com.

March 5

"I am grateful for myself and for my body. I am grateful for my ability to see and hear, feel and taste and touch."

~ Louise Hay

It is often difficult for us to be grateful about ourselves. We have learned from society to pluck this, dye that, tighten those, reduce, reshape, and shrink most of our "parts" (oops some we are to "enlarge". We can look good and be healthy; it also works so much better, if we are grateful for what we do and have and especially if it still works. Our body protects the very essence, our mind, our heart, spirit and soul, let us be kind to what allows us to transport the very essence of who we are.

Take a moment and be grateful for what your body, your physical senses have done for you today. Write down your gratitude for your body.

_____

_____

_____

_____

_____

_____

_____

_____

_____

_____

March 6

What is gratitude? Gratitude is a simple act of expressing appreciation or thankful thoughts for the good things which have happened to us. Unless we acknowledge our achievements, we will have no idea how far we have reached in our life. Expressing thankful thoughts and complaining are two opposite things that have its respective effects on our brain and in our life. WHILE complaining can make us feel powerless, expressing gratitude can give make us in charge of the situation. By acknowledging and affirming our gratitude, we can move ahead in any situation whereas complaining can make us stand still. If stress, anxiety, and depression are the dark forces in our life that pull us down, then gratitude is the counterforce that can make us feel calm and peaceful. If happiness is a state of mind, then gratitude is the way to achieve it. By simply exercising the act of being thankful every single morning a huge change in our outlook and mental health can occur. It's a conscious effort to be mindful and create the positive thoughts in our brain which can make us happy.

Mind you; Gratitude is a conscious habit.

Mansi Parmar was born and raised in India and settled in Canada. Mansi is a Biotechnologist, a Home Maker, and a Crafter. Connect with Mansi at Mansiparmar06@gmail.com.

March 7

"You simply will not be the same person two months from now after consciously giving thanks each day for the abundance that exists in your life. And you will have set in motion an ancient spiritual law: the more you have and are grateful for, the more will be given you."

~ Sarah Ban Breathnach

Live In Gratitude Daily can be started on any day of the year. This quote may be read after one month, two months, three months or perhaps you are almost done with a year of gratitude; notice the change within you from practicing and living gratitude. Do you see how your life has changed? If you are just starting, know you have a wonderful journey ahead of you.

What have you already gained by practicing, living and sharing gratitude?

_____

_____

_____

_____

_____

_____

_____

_____

_____

_____

_____

_____

March 8

"Can you see the holiness in those things you take for granted–a paved road or a washing machine? If you concentrate on finding what is good in every situation, you will discover that your life will suddenly be filled with gratitude, a feeling that nurtures the soul."

~ Rabbi Harold Kushner

Wherever you are right now, write about what you see and are grateful for? If it is hard to imagine, think about how life would be without it. (In this regard, I am thankful for toilet paper, never leave home without it!! I am also grateful for water and electricity).

_____

_____

_____

_____

_____

_____

_____

_____

_____

_____

_____

_____

_____

March 9

"I'm so grateful for all I've seen, in my great uncovering. Truth came in, pulled me apart, exposing my awakened heart."

~Bentley Kalaway

I once suffered a great disappointment which completely demolished my creative spirit. After several months of feeling diminished, I found myself sitting in a stream of sunlight asking for my creativity to return. I heard the lyrics written above at that moment. The lesson I learned that day is deeply ingrained now. Gratitude is a profound healer, especially on those occasions when huge grief or pain is uncovered; for times we feel completely pulled apart. Although we may temporarily turn our gaze away, a moment often arrives where our eyes are willing to look inward, to acknowledge the beauty that always remains. We feel our heart open and stretch as if it is just waking from a long rest. Expressing gratitude allows us to cushion a crisis when we fall, to build up our emotional and psychological immune systems to deal with the ups and downs inherent in life.

Bentley Kalaway *is a Singer/Songwriter, Author and Coach and an Evolutionary Beacon for the Emergence of the Empowered Embodied Feminine. She is passionate about supporting others to claim, amplify and act upon their inner wisdom for their fulfillment and our collective evolution. www.facebook.com/BentleyKalawayMusic.*

March 10

In Memory of Carmella Scarfo, Mother, Grandmother, Mentor, and Best Friend.

As a 50+ entrepreneur, only child, wife and mother of 3, the most memorable reflections of happiness and gratitude turn to my grandmother, Carmella. The unconditional love, friendship, and undying positive outlook is something that I strive to pursue and give to my children every day because of her.

As the first born grandchild, I was able to experience first-hand an unbreakable bond that shaped the outlook I have on life. She was the only constant in my life that was always there to support, nurture and accept me for who I am. Her infamous phrase uttered gently during times of chaos still echo in my head "It'll all work out". Simple words to some but issued by a strong person, and one who loved her family so deeply, they ring in my head daily as an inspiration to keep going and have faith in mankind.

Having faith in my God and repeating the words of Carmella has seen me through a tumultuous and devastating divorce, homelessness and financial ruin. However, emerging as a victor, strong and uber successful entrepreneur is credited to a woman named Carmella, whose words echo in my head daily.

So it is with a grateful heart and unsinkable pursuit of happiness, I offer these words to you in the voice of Carmella – "It'll all work out".

Karen A. Thomas is an Etiquette Educator, Speaker, Author, and Trainer. Known as the CT Etiquette Expert, she inspires people to be the most Poised, Polished and Professional in the business arena. A monthly segment contributor on NBC & ABC as well as CT radio. https://www.ctetiquette.com and ctetiquette@gmail.com.

March 11

"Gratitude is a thought so simple, it is almost effortless;
The abundance, joy, and love gained are limitless."

~ Denise Joy Thompson

If a daily practice can bring you your dreams, are you willing to do it?
If so, Live In Gratitude Daily. What is your daily gratitude practice?

_____

_____

_____

_____

_____

_____

_____

_____

_____

_____

_____

_____

March 12

MESSAGES + PATTERNS = GRATEFUL MIRACLES

This day is the birthday of my Godmother, my Aunt Eileen. More significantly, she has remained the longest, strongest, steadiest, and most steadfast friend throughout my life. Aptly named, I have leaned both on, and towards her many times. The gratitude I have for her, our bond, and the value she brings to my life is, truly, immeasurable. I encourage everyone to invest in at least one intergenerational relationship in their lifetime, ensuring it has meaningful depth and significance so that this connection can become a preserved legacy for evermore generations.

Coincidentally, this date also marks a day when I learned to stand – and stand tall – for something I believed in.

Have you ever had the feeling you were compelled to say "YES" to something – and didn't understand why? I am grateful I listened to the still, small voice that whispered, "You belong in Pittsburg". Today was the manifestation of acting upon that "YES"; which resulted in an exponential expansion of my circle of connections. Connections whereby we support MANY to ALL stand – stronger together!

Laurie Vallas delights in observing the patterns between people and events and drawing unconventional associations between the two. She particularly enjoys the challenge of transforming these opportunities into meaningful, influential connections. The pursuit of revealing 'the heartifacts' within everything has become the foundation of Laurie's work. Happy to connect on FB: The Heartifacts, PositiviTEAs or at theheartifacts@gmail.com

March 13

"We can be thankful to a friend for a few acres or a little money; and yet for the freedom and command of the whole earth, and for the great benefits of our being, our life, health, and reason, we look upon ourselves as under no obligation."

~ Marcus Annaeus Seneca

Be grateful for all we have and all we could have. The choice is ours to be grateful for our self and all we have access to.

Take a moment and think about all of the opportunities you have had today? All of the opportunities in your future. Which of these are you the most grateful for?

_____

_____

_____

_____

_____

_____

_____

_____

_____

_____

_____

_____

_____

March 14

"A diamond was born today, to shine and sparkle and give light,

walk with me, and hold my hand, feel the warmth of the light, feel the shine,

let's sparkle together you and I."

Theodora I. Prokopiw *is a College Student and lives in New Jersey.*

Who can you "sparkle" with? How do you shine, sparkle and give light to others?

_____

_____

_____

_____

_____

_____

_____

_____

_____

_____

_____

_____

_____

_____

March 15

"Gratitude is more of a compliment to yourself than someone else."

~ Raheel Farooq

What are the qualities we look for in others? We look for kindness, courtesy, appreciation; how are we doing in giving those to ourself and others?

What are your "gratitude qualities"? What do you recognize in yourself?

_____

_____

_____

_____

_____

_____

_____

_____

_____

_____

_____

_____

_____

_____

March 16

"Keep your eyes open and try to catch people in your company doing something right, then praise them for it."

~ Tom Hopkins

Appreciation and being grateful for what people do and rather than what people don't do reaps huge rewards. There is a story about a golf instructor teaching two groups of golfers. The first group was praised on everything they did right and encouraged to do those things again. The second group was told what was wrong and to correct it. Which group do you think did better? The second group right, since they corrected what was wrong? I know you have the answer…Yes, it was the first group. They were appreciated, encouraged, and they could focus on the positive. This book helps you focus on the positive, YOUR positive gratitude!! Your practice of gratitude, appreciation, and thankfulness for yourself and others will grow because we are concentrating on it.

What did you do right today and how are you grateful for it?

_____

_____

_____

_____

_____

_____

_____

_____

_____

_____

March 17

In Dedication to Mom and Dad

Thank you for never hindering my strong will or drive to be creative.

Thank you for being at every single game or dance recital.

Thank you for **STILL** continuing to support me, my husband and our amazing family.

Thank you for raising me with good morals, a desire to help others, and a conviction to right the injustices that are wrong in this world.

Thank you for ensuring that I was raised in the Church.

Thank you for giving us the freedom to make our own mistakes as children and for teaching us how to lose. Even more so for teaching us not to quit after we lose, but to learn from it and become better.

Thank you for being so open with your love and never failing to give it in abundance.

Thank you for being the perfect parents for me.

"Train up a child in the way he should go: and when he is old, he will not depart from it."
~Proverbs 22:6

I pray daily to be half the parents you are.

Brittany L. Sumner *is a Wife to a wonderful husband, Mother to a rambunctious son and Business Owner at* www.crazywinelady.com. *She has a passion for helping others, serving her church and enjoying a good glass of wine.*

_____

_____

_____

_____

_____

_____

_____

_____

_____

_____

March 18

Gratitude has become a buzzword and can almost seem like a trend. Yet when we truly feel grateful our life can be transformed in so many ways. The key for me has always been to push myself to be grateful for things that don't always seem worthy of gratitude. I've been grateful for a speeding ticket, an illness, and a challenging time in my life. Why gratitude during those times? Tough times are actually an opportunity for me to learn and grow and to see what opportunity those challenges bring. An illness has allowed me time to evaluate the pace of my life but also to be grateful for the times that I am healthy. A speeding ticket reminds me to get more conscious throughout the day. It's easy to be grateful for the great things in our life but finding gratitude for the tough times can be an interesting and mind shifting opportunity for change. Try it and see how you do.

Lisa Kaplin *is a Psychologist, Life Coach and the Owner of Smart Women Inspired Lives. She is the married and the mother of three young-adult children. You can reach her at Lisa@smartwomeninspiredlives.com and www.smartwomeninspiredlives.com.*

_____

_____

_____

_____

_____

_____

_____

_____

_____

_____

_____

March 19

"In life, one has a choice to take one of two paths: to wait for some special day--or to celebrate each special day."

~ Rasheed Ogunlaru

Gratitude is celebrating big and small achievements, behaviors, occasions, task completion, anything which happens can be a cause for celebration…or what didn't happen. As I am writing this, I think of potty training (ironic since I do not have children), each occasion of "successful" behavior can be celebrated. Clapping our hands, praising the child, being happy with them, this results in them having fun during this often trying period of child development. Let's make everything fun and a celebration!! Let's reward ourselves for completing our "get-to-do list" (I do not call it a "to-do list"). I am blessed to have a list, to have tasks, to have things to do.

What can you be grateful for today and how will you celebrate it?

_____

_____

_____

_____

_____

_____

_____

_____

_____

_____

_____

_____

March 20

4 Steps to a ***Grateful*** Heart
1) Pray
2) Give Thanks
3) Affirm
4) Repeat

"Let us be grateful to people who make us happy; they are the charming gardeners who make our souls bloom."
~ Marcel Proust

Lori Ann Foster *is a Consultant, Coach, and Mentor with a background in healthcare and professional coaching. She is passionate about personal development, resiliency of the human spirit and living from a place of gratitude. Connect with Lori at contact@lorifostercoaching.com and* www.lorifostercoaching.com.

March 21

In Honor of River's Birthday! You are My Special Buffalo Girl Always!

Thankfulness, this word is so poignant in my life. I was reading some of my dreams from 2014. I was walking through the fire and facing my shadows. I was surrounded by you who loved me in Sedona, the great Spirits of Quetzalcoatl in Teo and all those present after my brother's passing in July when I emerged at The Place of the Women. I was pulled literally from my brink of destruction to a life and dream I had only imagined. I am very grateful for all who love me every day and who receive my love as my heart is so open. I am thankful for my trials in life as they have taught me to face adversity and made me a Warrior. I am now a servant in this life, and I serve as hope and an example of courage and total surrender and what it looks like. I now claim to know nothing and show up in the present moment fully alive.

I choose to Live In Gratitude Daily.

Laura Goodman The Shameless Warrior(tm) is the embodiment of reverent authentic love. Her mission is to lend her voice to Warriors of abuse who have not found theirs. Laura is an Author, Mentor, Warrior, Teacher, Speaker, Advocate. She is here to serve humanity and loves with an open heart, fully and completely. Connect with Laura at www.facebook.com/pg/shamelesswarrior

March 22

In Honor of My Son David's Birthday, My Pride and Joy

I allow life to flow through me and never stop the energy of the consciousness of the universe. I live in love, not fear. I consciously choose where I want to be, with whom I spend time. I am thankful for my mother and for all that she taught me. I am who I am because I chose to be resilient and spirited rather than give up when I was in my dark moments. I am so grateful for my family and our health. My beloved wife and for the mountains I wake up to every day. I feel blessed just to be able to breathe and be sober one day at a time. To be teachable with an open heart is my continued wish for my life. To share my love with all who cross my path is my way to raise the global consciousness and promote healing on this planet. This is the prayer in my heart.

Love to all of you!

Laura Goodman *The Shameless Warrior(tm) is the embodiment of reverent authentic love. Her mission is to lend her voice to Warriors of abuse who have not found theirs. Laura is an Author, Mentor, Warrior, Teacher, Speaker, and Advocate. She is here to serve humanity and loves with an open heart, fully and completely. Connect with Laura at* www.facebook.com/pg/shamelesswarrior

_____

_____

_____

_____

_____

_____

_____

_____

_____

_____

March 23

"This a wonderful day. I've never seen this one before."

~ Maya Angelou

There is a saying "any day I wake up is a good day". We **can** make it a good day!! It will be a good day if we are grateful for opening our eyes, for being alive, for breathing. I know at times there are trials and tribulations in our lives; with a Live In Gratitude Daily habit, we can see and feel even the smallest glimmer of gratitude and fan the smoldering flames to make it into a roaring fire, heating not only our hearts but the hearts of those around us. We want the flames of gratitude to light up our life and the lives of those we come into contact with. Yes, the future's so bright I gotta wear shades, kind of a feeling!!

On this wonderful day, what and who are you grateful for?

_____

_____

_____

_____

_____

_____

_____

_____

_____

_____

_____

March 24

It is often said that when you are feeling down or inadequate, one way to change the feeling is to ask yourself, "What am I grateful for?" or "What could I be grateful for?"

For me, when this happens, I think about my senses: like being grateful for my eyesight, my hearing, my senses of touch, smell and taste. I begin to feel different and move away from me to people who have helped me in life, like my wife, mom, dad and children. Then a sense of humility comes over me, revealing that I don't do life alone. My life has been blessed with so many wondrous opportunities, beloved gifts, and amazing adventures. It is only right that I pass on my gratefulness to you and let you know that you are appreciated. You are special and in your times of struggle or when you find yourself feeling wronged, know that I am grateful for you.

Because you're reading this message, I get to pass on my gift - for that I am grateful.

*Award winning expert, certified coach and author, **Kevin V. Huhn**, chased his boyhood dream from the age of five until it was realized nearly 40 years later. He overcame odds and realized that his succeeding needed the help of others. Connect with Kevin at KevinHuhn.com*

March 25

Today is The Day that I Married My Best Friend and The Love of My life!
These quotes were written by my husband, Hayward, for our wedding announcement and still hold true many years later.

"Our relationship has blossomed and grown through tremendous challenges, and we express our thanks for the support we have received from all the family and friends who will receive this announcement."

"To bend without breaking and flow without boundaries toward our source together."

As I write this my heart is full of love and feels the way it did on our beautiful wedding day. The tears of happiness are here, just as on that day. Isn't it amazing how this feeling stays alive in my heart?

I am forever grateful for the day we met and the journey we are on together!!

Shannon Gaude is a Co-owner of Hayward Gaude Photography Portrait and Design Studio. Connect with Shannon at shannon@haywardgaudephotography.com and www.haywardgaudephotography.com

_____

_____

_____

_____

_____

_____

_____

_____

_____

_____

March 26

> *"Walk as if you are kissing the Earth with your feet."*

~ *Thich Nhat Hanh*

We need to be in love with each day. When we **Live In Gratitude Daily**, we greet the sun in the morning with a smile on our face, excited to start our day, knowing we are grateful for who and what we have in our life.

What are you grateful each morning when you wake up?

_____

_____

_____

_____

_____

_____

_____

_____

_____

_____

_____

_____

_____

_____

_____

March 27

"Do not spoil what you have by desiring what you have not; remember that what you now have was once among the things you only hoped for."

~ Epicurus

This quote spoke to me, brought tears to my eyes. (Reading many heartfelt gratitude quotes will do that). By desiring (coveting) what we do not have, this takes away the joy of our present moment. This does not mean we do not work for what we want, gratitude for what we have and taking action helps us to achieve more. In gratitude for what I have, I am able to move forward and receive.

Take a moment and think about what you have been "desiring"? Now take a moment and write down what you are grateful for this present moment, this moment of your life and "see" what you have. Accept what is now and then move forward in gratitude, open to receive what will come of your actions.

_____

_____

_____

_____

_____

_____

_____

_____

_____

_____

March 28

"When you have a good friend that really cares for you and tries to stick in there with you, you treat them like nothing. Learn to be a good friend because one day you're gonna look up and say I lost a good friend. Learn how to be respectful to your friends, don't just start arguments with them and don't tell them the reason, always remember your friends will be there quicker than your family. Learn to remember you got great friends, don't forget that and they will always care for you no matter what. Always remember to smile and look up at what you got in life."

~ Marilyn Monroe

(I think you may be surprised to see a quote from Marilyn Monroe in this journal.*)* Marilyn does have a message, a message of being grateful for who we have in our life and showing appreciation to them. I know at times I have been so busy, I do not show or share my appreciation of those I care for. There are excuses not to call, not to "write/text", not to spend time with them; work, tired, busy, is this familiar to anyone?

Who are you grateful for and how can you show/tell them you appreciate them?

_____

_____

_____

_____

_____

_____

_____

_____

_____

_____

_____

March 29

"True forgiveness is when you can say, Thank you for that experience."

~ Oprah Winfrey

This is a very profound statement. If we "thank" anyone and everyone for experiences and lessons we did not want, this is a sign of maturity and enlightenment. I see this as also thanking and releasing our self from holding onto what happened. We are thanking our self for accepting and embracing the lesson. I see forgiveness of others as also forgiving our self for holding onto the story, the blame, the negativity. It does not negate any wrong which was committed; it allows us to let go and move forward.

What lessons or experiences are you now grateful for which at the time (or for a while now) **you had not accepted and moved forward from?**

_____

_____

_____

_____

_____

_____

_____

_____

_____

_____

March 30

"Reward yourself for all you do
No matter how big or how small.
Celebrate You and
Be Grateful for Your Action."

~ Denise Joy Thompson

What are your "wins" today? What did you accomplish? What went right or at least not wrong? Celebrate something every day. Every day is worth celebrating!!

_____

_____

_____

_____

_____

_____

_____

_____

_____

_____

_____

March 31

Dedicated to my sister, Susan King, and my brother, James Anthony Day, Jr.

I have truly been blessed with my sister and brother. My sister, Susan, has been an amazing role model. She has taught me to be selfless in raising children and supporting family. I don't have children, but my sister has three. Those children have brought me some of the greatest joys of my life. Seeing life through their eyes has given me an appreciation for the simplest things making me smile. Now they have children of their own, and I have the opportunity to witness the beauty of seeing the generations evolve. This is the gift of my sister. I express gratitude to her regularly for allowing me the privilege of being with children. My brother, Jim, is an athlete and hard worker. His constant drive and motivation to be the best at every endeavor have influenced me in ways I couldn't imagine. He never gives up; my brother is like a rock, strong and beautiful at the same time. My siblings have filled my life with unconditional love. I am fully appreciative of the impact they have had in my life. I have been rewarded to live wonderful moments vicariously through them. For this, I live in gratitude now and for all eternity…

Jean Day has a Master's degree in Clinical Psychology from Pepperdine University, is a college instructor, for 18 years, and a guest expert on numerous radio shows discussing topics about psychology and wellness. Jean is a Nichiren Buddhist and a member of the Soka-Gakkai USA Buddhist organization. Contact Jean at jeanday319@yahoo.com.

"Appreciation of someone's efforts,
creates a smile, a warming of their heart and
a lasting impression of your kindness."

~ *Denise Joy Thompson*

*"Thank you is a "miracle" phrase
which changes the moment forever."*

~ Denise Joy Thompson

April

 **April 1**

PERSISTENCE IN THE PURSUIT OF HAPPINESS & HOW IT CIRCLED BACK TO GRATITUDE

I'd heard of 'The Happiness Project' whilst living overseas, in a place where I couldn't imagine feeling any happier. Happiness, and the pursuit of it can be as captivating and alluring as the ability to define the Origin of Being.

A GREAT-FULL STORY:

A friend photographs unfettered nature daily, and consistently shares these photos on an email list of broad, anonymous membership. I introduce another friend to this work; who is moved to purchase a piece. The same photo is featured in a magazine. I drive to a bookshop to purchase the magazine – and stumble across 'The Happiness Project – One Sentence/ Five-Year Journal". I recall the author is speaking locally that night. I purchase the book and attend the event to listen and meet the author. While in line, I am asked what brought me there, and I share my story. The woman who asked **belongs** to that photograph email list and is suddenly no longer anonymous. She shares her gratitude for the 'no-longer-anonymous' photographers. I share the feedback with my friend; completing the circle.

__Laurie Vallas__ delights in observing the patterns between people and events and drawing unconventional associations between the two. She particularly enjoys the challenge of transforming these opportunities into meaningful, influential connections. The pursuit of revealing 'the heartifacts' within everything has become the foundation of Laurie's work. Happy to connect on FB: The Heartifacts, PositiviTEAs or at: theheartifacts@gmail.com

April 2

"When we become more fully aware that our success is due in large measure to the loyalty, helpfulness, and encouragement we have received from others, our desire grows to pass on similar gifts. Gratitude spurs us on to prove ourselves worthy of what others have done for us. The spirit of gratitude is a powerful energizer."

~ Wilferd A. Peterson

What have you received (in gratitude) from others? How have you shown your gratitude and How do you pass it on?

_____

_____

_____

_____

_____

_____

_____

_____

_____

_____

_____

_____

_____

April 3

"Whatever our individual troubles and challenges may be, it's important to pause every now and then to appreciate all that we have, on every level. We need to literally "count our blessings," give thanks for them, allow ourselves to enjoy them, and relish the experience of prosperity we already have."

~ Shakti Gawain

Life is very hectic, overwhelming and sometimes it may seem more than one can bear. Even in our darkest moments, we can find a glimmer of "gratitude". To find the glimmer, we need to take a moment, breathe, quiet our mind and be open to receive what God, our Higher Power, the Universe, or someone is going to give to us.

What we are given is the "glimmer."

What are you grateful for, even in the face of adversity?

_____

_____

_____

_____

_____

_____

_____

_____

_____

_____

_____

April 4

"Thou that has given so much to me,
Give one thing more–a grateful heart;
Not thankful when it pleaseth me,
As if thy blessings had spare days;
But such a heart, whose pulse may be
Thy praise."

~ George Herbert

"Not thankful when it pleaseth me," a grateful heart, a grateful habit is one which is with us 99% of the time. I say 99% because as humans, we are going to have those moments, what if those moments are rare, many months apart? What if we became used to grateful, that it is our nature? What would our world be like if everyone walked and talked in gratitude? It is almost unimaginable, we all would work together for the common good, and we all would be filled with abundance, joy, and love.

For now, only each one of us can do our part, have a grateful heart for 99% of the time.

For your 99% of the day, what are you grateful for?

_____

_____

_____

_____

_____

_____

_____

_____

_____

April 5

"(Some people) have a wonderful capacity to appreciate again and again, freshly and naively, the basic goods of life, with awe, pleasure, wonder, and even ecstasy."

~ A.H. Maslow

I was fortunate during my deployments, though I visited "bare" bases, I was usually at bases with many amenities. Amenities of hot and cold water, a wonderful dining facility, hardened buildings, electricity (sometimes intermittent). Nothing to the standards of being in the US, having those "basic goods of life" was appreciated. For a few weeks the water was not usable; what does this mean? It meant bottled water showers, this is what some people were using at their locations all the time, and they were grateful for the bottled water. When we were able to use the hot and cold water again, I greatly appreciated that convenience, something often taken for granted.

What are the "basic goods of life" that you are grateful for? What do you have now that you are grateful for?

_____

_____

_____

_____

_____

_____

_____

_____

_____

_____

_____

April 6

"Find the good and praise it."

~ Alex Haley

Gratitude is best experienced by acknowledging it, expressing it, sharing it. The song, "This Little Light Of Mine" (which I sang on stage one time during a transformational retreat), came to mind as I read this quote. Like the light, gratitude is meant to shine; we want people to know we are grateful, we appreciate, we are thankful.

Gratitude is not meant to be hidden; it is meant to be lived and to be shared so others also can enjoy being grateful.

With our "lighted candle of gratitude," we can light the candles of gratitude for others.

With whom have you expressed or shared your gratitude? How was this experience for you?

_____

_____

_____

_____

_____

_____

_____

_____

_____

_____

_____

_____

April 7

"What if you gave someone a gift, and they neglected to thank you for it would you be likely to give them another? Life is the same way. In order to attract more of the blessings that life has to offer, you must truly appreciate what you already have."

~ Ralph Marston

When I appreciate the basics or what might be considered insignificant things (for us in the US), I feel this openness and lightness within me. I am not bogged down by wanting, the fact my computer works, the heat is on, (or the AC as needed), I have a refrigerator, a microwave, a washer and dryer. Not everyone has these same "basics". In my early days as a social worker, I worked with non-profit agencies providing health care and social services for the families who were homeless and low-income, I do not discount what I have, for I have seen those with less who were appreciative of what they had, which was a lot less than me. I also noticed those who were appreciative of the services provided and who were thankful to be given assistance to move forward in their life, actually made progress in becoming self-sufficient, those who angry and bitter did not seem to be able to move forward. We are all in a certain place in our life, we can stay stagnate, or we recognize and appreciate what we have in the current moment and in doing so are open to moving forward and receiving more.

What are you grateful to have right now, even as you are moving forward in building the life you want to create?

_____

_____

_____

_____

_____

_____

_____

_____

April 8

"There is a calmness to a life lived in gratitude, a quiet joy."

~ Ralph H. Blum

Gratitude allows us to be aware of what is right, leaving little time to focus on what is wrong. When we are appreciative and grateful for the big and the small, "imperfections" don't bother us.

Take a moment and think about what gratitude has brought to your life, are you calmer, more loving, happier, more content, more joyful, and playful? Write about how you feel about what gratitude has brought to your life.

_____

_____

_____

_____

_____

_____

_____

_____

_____

_____

_____

_____

_____

_____

April 9

"The moment one gives close attention to anything, even a blade of grass, it becomes a mysterious, awesome, indescribably magnificent world in itself."

~ Henry Miller

In the past, you might not have thought much about what you give your attention to. This is a very important part of how to Live In Gratitude Daily. By giving close attention to gratitude, appreciation and giving thanks, our lives become awesome, indescribably magnificent lives.

What aspect of gratitude are you giving your attention to? How do you see your life changing due to the gratitude you are experiencing, sharing, giving and even receiving?

_____

_____

_____

_____

_____

_____

_____

_____

_____

_____

_____

_____

_____

_____

April 10

"Gratefulness is the key to a happy life that we hold in our hands, because if we are not grateful, then no matter how much we have we will not be happy — because we will always want to have something else or something more."

~ Brother David Steindl-Rast

Research show gratefulness does increase the level of happiness, actually Gratitude is the foundation for more happiness, joy, love, health, wealth, many things which we all want stem from Gratitude.

How are you creating more Gratitude in your life? What are you focusing on, what are you thinking, how are you appreciating and thanking others? What are you noticing about yourself with gratitude?

_____

_____

_____

_____

_____

_____

_____

_____

_____

_____

_____

_____

_____

April 11

I was in 7th grade the first time I fell in love. I didn't know he was very ill, yet every day during one beautiful summer he'd stand at the end of his driveway to say "hi".

One afternoon he called me over, "Will you be my girlfriend?", he whispered. "Yes," I said. "We have to kiss now," he moved closer, and we did. A gentle, lingering, sweet kiss. "You can't forget me now you know." I shook my head, "I won't." "Promise?" "Promise."

I never saw him after that day. I learned a few months later he passed away, his fight with terminal cancer over.

His memory is still with me 40 years later. When I get so busy or involved in something that I begin to neglect loved ones, his memory calls me to remember life is fleeting. It's precious, and everyone in our lives deserves to know we love them and aren't forgetting them. First loves aren't always as lasting, but I'm so grateful the memory of mine remains.

Judith Richardson Schroeder, *a Sub-conscious Behaviorist and Life Enhancement Coach, helps clients uncover their inner gifts and teaches them how to foster a life of true gratitude and fulfillment. Her favorite pastime though is spending time with her beautiful granddaughter, Arya. Connect with Judith at www.guidancefromwithincoaching.com.*

April 12

"Bring to mind someone you care about, someone it is easy to rejoice for. Picture them and feel the natural joy you have for their well-being, for their happiness and success. With each breath, offer them your grateful, heartfelt wishes:

May you be joyful.
May your happiness increase.
May you not be separated from great happiness.
May your good fortune and the causes for your joy and happiness increase.

Sense the sympathetic joy and caring in each phrase. When you feel some degree of natural gratitude for the happiness of this loved one, extend this practice to another person you care about. Recite the same simple phrases that express your heart's intention."

~ Jack Kornfield

The simple act of thinking about someone and silently or out loud expressing gratitude, joy, and love for them instantly increases our gratitude, joy and love. Our thoughts are so powerful and create energy within us. The more "gratitude energy" we create, the more we have in our life.

Who is on your "send gratitude thoughts" to list? Write down their names and send the thoughts written above.

_____

_____

_____

_____

_____

_____

_____

_____

_____

April 13

Disappointment or Gift?

I think about the dreams and visions I held when I was younger. I see now how my life path did not so closely follow many of my younger ideas. In hindsight now, I have immense gratitude for the wisdom that guided me into and through other life choices.

So often it has seemed that every fall, every disappointment, every stumble, and every shortcoming I experienced is like riding out a rough storm at sea in a small boat. I felt tossed and turned about in all directions, and at times, I barely knew which way is up. But I'll stay the course, grateful for the boon of a worthy vessel and the stamina to continue. When the storm lets up and calm seas again prevail? Who knows yet whether I will be further away, or perhaps even closer to the core of my heart's desire. The gift, I believe, is in deciding which it is. Either way, I'll be grateful for the day, the exhilaration of life, my breath and the beautiful, unique fabric of my life.

Wendy Whitney Harbath enjoys Ceremony, Sacred Listening, and being in tune with the Wild Inner Wise Woman; imbued with desire for connecting to the Light and all Benevolent Spirits everywhere. Connect at www.facebook.com/WendyWhitneyHarbath.

April 14

In Dedication to All Children

I knew at a very young age I was adopted. I do not remember feeling unloved, unwanted or out of place. My parents clearly loved me and wanted me, as they did my adopted brother. I met the social worker who placed me with my parents, and I ended up working for the same agency as an adoption specialist; I later incorporated adoption services into private practice. I remember my first baby, a girl; I picked up from the hospital from her birth mother. I had the experience of "me" being given to my loving mother from another loving mother. The experience was so surreal, and I knew I was to experience that moment, knew the love from my birth mother and the love I was to have with my forever family. That night I met my parents for dinner, the day's events unknown when scheduled. I told them about my experience, and we all had tears of love and joy for remembering my being given to them. This date in 1967, two years after being with my parents, my adoption was finalized. I am forever grateful for my family.

Denise Joy Thompson is a Wife, Mother of 3 furbabies, a #1 International Best-Selling Author, Coach, Colonel in the Air Force Reserve, a Therapist, and Veteran. She is the host of The Power Of A Woman's Voice TV show. Denise's mission is for all women to have a "voice". Connect with Denise at thecoachalliance@gmail.com and www.facebook.com/groups/liveingratitudedaily.

April 15

"As each day comes to us refreshed and anew, so does my gratitude renew itself daily. The breaking of the sun over the horizon is my grateful heart dawning upon a blessed world."

~ Adabella Radici

Every day is a great day to be grateful, to **Live In Gratitude Daily**. There will always be something to be grateful for; we often are programmed to look for what is wrong, instead of looking for what is "right". Refresh your thinking to always look for the good first, as you practice this; you will find it isn't even necessary to know what is wrong.

Write down what was good about this day and what you are grateful for?

_____

_____

_____

_____

_____

_____

_____

_____

_____

_____

_____

_____

April 16

"But the value of gratitude does not consist solely in getting you more blessings in the future. Without gratitude you cannot long keep from dissatisfied thought regarding things as they are."

~ Wallace Wattles

How often have we wanted something or someone and then after a few weeks, a few months or a few years, we realized the "who" or what wasn't what we wanted? If we are not grateful for what we have today, how can we be grateful and satisfied with what we get tomorrow? Being grateful for what we have now, opens our heart, mind, and soul to receive what we want, by being content with where we are now.

What are you grateful for right now and do not need to trade it for the "next better model"? What is working for you and you do not need the "newest shiny object"?

_____

_____

_____

_____

_____

_____

_____

_____

_____

_____

_____

_____

April 17

"Blessed are those that can give without remembering and receive without forgetting."

~ Author Unknown

Gratitude is not only about being content and satisfied with what we have it is about giving, appreciating, and thanking those who are in our lives. Giving gratitude to others regardless of appreciation or response is a true gift of gratitude we give our self. When we are in true gratitude of and for our self, we do not need recognition from others; we accept recognition when it is given with an open heart, though no recognition is required or sought. When we receive, we are double-blessed, and in gratitude, it is etched upon our heart.

In thinking back over your life, who are especially grateful to for the "gifts" they have given you. Did you thank them, if not can you do it now?

_____

_____

_____

_____

_____

_____

_____

_____

_____

_____

_____

April 18

"Nothing that is done for you is a matter of course. Everything originates in a will for the good, which is directed at you. Train yourself never to put off the word or action for the expression of gratitude."

~ Albert Schweitzer

We can accept good is intended for us all the time. Bad is not created by God or the Universe. Another person can create "bad", though all that is intended by our Higher Power is good. Always be prepared to be grateful and to express it, increasing our "seeing" and acceptance of good.

How are you expressing, sharing and living your gratitude? Are you more aware and expressing more often? What has changed for you by "doing" more gratitude?

_____

_____

_____

_____

_____

_____

_____

_____

_____

_____

_____

_____

_____

April 19

"God gave you a gift of 86,400 seconds today. Have you used one to say 'thank you?"

~ William A. Ward

Did you realize that is how many seconds in one day?

How many did you use today in being grateful? Was there any way to have used even more? What can you do tomorrow to use more "Live In Gratitude Daily seconds"?

_____

_____

_____

_____

_____

_____

_____

_____

_____

_____

_____

_____

_____

_____

_____

April 20

"Gratitude is a vaccine, an antitoxin, and an antiseptic."

~ John Henry Jowett

Gratitude and the mindset it creates can ward off many ills and has even cured some. In *Love, Medicine and Miracles* (Bernie S. Siegel) talks about the power of the mind (mindset) to cure cancer.

Think about the changes in your mood, your health, your relationships, how are they more positive and healthy than before your "Live In Gratitude Daily habit"?

_____

_____

_____

_____

_____

_____

_____

_____

_____

_____

_____

_____

_____

April 21

"Feeling grateful or appreciative of someone or something in your life actually attracts more of the things that you appreciate and value into your life."

~ *Christiane Northrup*

What we focus on grows. If I want to be healthier, I read about health, watch health shows and go to the gym. If I want to be closer to God, I go to church or a Bible study; if I want to be more in tune with nature, then I go for a walk, hike and spend time outdoors.

Regarding growing your gratitude, then join up with others who live and practice gratitude. Join the Live in Gratitude FB group to share and grow with others.

What are you doing differently to bring more gratitude into your life? Where are you spending time and with whom? Are there particular people you are spending more time with because they are practicing gratitude also?

_____

_____

_____

_____

_____

_____

_____

_____

_____

_____

April 22

"Love yourself first, and everything else falls into line. You really have to love yourself to get anything done in this world." – Lucille Ball

It's so easy for me to look in the mirror and notice all the things that I don't like...creeping crow's feet, a pesky pimple, extra weight in the wrong places. The critical voice of "me" demands my attention and often starts playing like a broken record. I've found what helps me the most is practicing a concept I learned from Louise Hay called Mirror Work. Stand in front of the mirror and say, "I love every inch of my body just as it is right now." In addition to telling yourself eye to eye in the mirror how much you love every inch of your body, focus on your FABulous features- the ones that you love.

When I look in the mirror, I am grateful to see _____.

Allison "FAB" Howell- Social Worker by day, Life Stylist by night teaching women to feel FABulous in Life & Style. Allison combines experience in fashion and psychology to inspire lives to be fun, fresh, and full of FABulous love. www.FABover.com.

_____

_____

_____

_____

_____

_____

_____

_____

_____

_____

_____

April 23

"Reflect upon your present blessings, of which every man has plenty;
not on your past misfortunes of which all men have some."

~ Charles Dickens

Reflecting on blessings and being grateful for them are tied together, counting our blessings without the gratitude attached, does not change our mindset. Gratitude is taking the "count your blessings" one step further, the step needed to change your mindset and consistent gratitude can actually "rewire" our brain.

How often are you reflecting on your blessings, what you have, what you have accomplished and truly getting in touch with the emotion/feeling of being grateful for what you have in your life? **What are the "blessings" in your life and how do you feel about them?**

_____

_____

_____

_____

_____

_____

_____

_____

_____

_____

_____

_____

April 24

"Both abundance and lack exist simultaneously in our lives, as parallel realities. It is always our conscious choice which secret garden we will tend… when we choose not to focus on what is missing from our lives but are grateful for the abundance that's present — love, health, family, friends, work, the joys of nature and personal pursuits that bring us pleasure — the wasteland of illusion falls away and we experience Heaven on earth."

~ Sarah Ban Breathnach

This is so true and is congruent with an earlier statement, what we focus on grows. What have you been tending to in your secret garden and is it time to make sure gratitude is growing over discontentment and desiring what we do not have?

What is abundant in your garden which you can be grateful for? Is there a person whom you can thank for your abundance? Including yourself?

_____

_____

_____

_____

_____

_____

_____

_____

_____

_____

_____

April 25

"Whenever we are appreciative, we are filled with a sense of well-being and swept up by the feeling of joy."

~ M.J. Ryan

I cannot fully explain the joy I have received from compiling and collaborating with all of the co-authors to create this journal. I am filled with such emotion and gratitude for what I have been experiencing. I am not untouched by reading and writing about gratitude; I realize I now, more than ever need to live what I am creating, reading and sharing with others. I am learning to Live In Gratitude Daily, and I look forward to continuing this journey with all of the readers and doers of this journal.

What have you learned the most about yourself as you have been practicing and living in gratitude? What are you the most grateful for since being on this journey?

_____

_____

_____

_____

_____

_____

_____

_____

_____

_____

_____

_____

April 26

"When you go deeply into the present, gratitude arises spontaneously, even if it's just gratitude for breathing, gratitude for the aliveness that you feel in your body. Gratitude is there when you acknowledge the aliveness of the present moment."

~ Eckhart Tolle

Gratitude can be experienced with every breath we take, every thought can be one of gratitude for what we have, what happened or didn't happen, what we choose to do or what we chose not to do. "I think therefore I am" can be, "I think therefore I am grateful". We can choose this, practice this, live this; live in gratitude daily.

What do you feel... when you take a moment just to be present, just take a deep breathe and be, quiet your thoughts, quiet your mind, feel your breath, just be. Feel the peace...feel you, feel gratitude.

April 27

In Dedication to My Husband of 20+ years

Today is our anniversary. It's an especially fine day to express gratitude. Just over a year ago my husband was able to quit a full-time job he didn't love to come work with me full time. Gratitude has played a powerful role in our ongoing success in life and marriage. Saying thank you for the small gifts, touches, and ideas. Saying thank you for the love, help, and support.

I feel grateful even for the days that are challenging when there is too much to do, and we are juggling our business and life with two busy teenagers.

If you want to create more happiness in your marriage or more abundance in your business, look for opportunities to express gratitude daily. I wake up each morning and lie in bed and focus on what I am grateful for. I know firsthand that a daily practice of expressing gratitude will change your life and lead to your dreams coming true. What can you express gratitude for today?

Minette Riordan, Ph.D. is an Award-winning Entrepreneur, Best-selling Author, Wife, Mom, Artist, and Foodie. Ready to manifest more money in your business and have fun doing it? Download Minette's gift of Money, Meditation & Mandalas at www.PathtoProfitAcademy.com/mmm

April 28

"Gratitude is riches. Complaint is poverty."

–Doris Day

What comes to mind is how this quote fits into the song I remember most sung by Doris Day? (Hmmm…depending on the age of the reader, this might not be familiar), that is Que sera sera, whatever will be will be, the future's not ours to see, so que sera, sera. We do not know the future, we know today, and we know what we have and what we can be grateful for, wanting/desiring what we do not have will not create the future we want, nor will complaints of today. Our Live In Gratitude Daily habit creates a today we are happy with and through the gratitude of and for today, the positive energy we create will attract a positive future. Focus on today, focus on gratitude.

When looking through the eyes of gratitude, what are your riches? What are you blessed with?

_____

_____

_____

_____

_____

_____

_____

_____

_____

_____

April 29

"Many people who order their lives rightly in all other ways are kept in poverty by their lack of gratitude."

~ Wallace Wattles

How many lottery winners have spent all of their winnings, ended up bankrupt and even homeless?   What was the mindset they had before winning which did not allow them to keep what they had won? How often do we see someone win an award, land a job, marry the person of our dreams? Then it seems they are not able to live what they now have, some do very well, and others seems to crash and burn; as if because of their mindset they could not live up to what they had received.

How are you increasing your gratitude? Here are a few actions to take, write down if this has happened today:

Thanking your family members for completing tasks? Thanking your co-workers for working with you? Thanking the cashier or wait staff? Thanking yourself for getting through the day in gratitude?

_____

_____

_____

_____

_____

_____

_____

_____

_____

April 30

To My Children, The Joy of My Life, Raymond and Gaby

I was blessed whit my two beautiful children at the right time of my life. Raymond, fragile and yet strong you came to me first at a time in my life when I was lost, felt unloved and incapable of loving anyone or even myself. You, my son, have taught me to love!

My sweet, beautiful girl, you brought so many experiences for us, the good the bad and the ugly and yet, we prevailed. Gaby girl God blessed me with your presence when my life had no meaning, no beginning or end. You, my love, taught me to love myself.

"What a child doesn't receive, it could seldom later give".
~ R.D. James

Claudia Nava *is a Wife and Mother of 2 children who loves to have fun and laugh!! She owns two businesses, Claudia Cleaning Services and a direct sales team with Stream. Connect with Claudia at yoko4you.mystream.com.*

"Embrace your ability to change your world and the world of those around you by being grateful for the moment of awakening and the moment of sleep, ending a great day."

~ Denise Joy Thompson

May

May 1

REPEAT this affirmation 20 times: Every Day in Every Way; I am getting Better & Better *(Affirmation by Dr. Émile Coué)*

JOURNAL: create 3 columns DEMONSTRATION— ELIMINATION —GRATITUDE

DEMONSTRATION—what is it that you want to Create…Demonstrate…Manifest?

ELIMINATION—interestingly—almost instantly after declaring what you WANT, the head plays tricks with negative tapes, self-doubts, today's worries, etc. Write down every negative that comes up no matter how strange in the elimination column.

CANCEL-CANCEL: by the end of the day, take a RED marker and write CANCEL, CANCEL in BIG BLOCK letters across each 'negative core thought' on your elimination column. Cancel out all negativity from your page—from your consciousness, and then— eliminate IT today and do not bring IT back tomorrow!

GRATITUDE—Thanks And Grow Rich! Gratitude and negativity cannot occupy the same space, so once your negativity is eliminated, you now have an opportunity to give Thanks And Grow Rich! Back to what you want? You don't have to know the HOW, just WHAT!

Jane A. Heron is a Keynote Speaker, a Podcasting Coach, and the Gutsy GURU at www.ThanksAndGrowRich.com.

_____

_____

_____

_____

_____

_____

_____

_____

_____

May 2

In Memory of My Mom, Anna Ruth Grimes

As a life coach, I am grateful for the awareness of how important gratitude is to success and happiness. I am grateful for my ability to experience this positive energy force. I know that a grateful state of mind creates a kind, happy and abundant life.

Gratitude is one of the most powerful energy forces in the universe.

Three things I am grateful for:
1. **Myself-** I know that I am worthy of magnificent things. And I am good enough just the way I am. I am so grateful to be me.
2. **Other people-** I know that I need other people to survive in this world. I am grateful to have amazing family and friends.
3. **Life-** I love the saying "You have one life, and this is not a trial run". If you don't appreciate what you have why should life give you any more? Life is abundantly in everything I am grateful to be living.

Of course, there many more things that I am grateful for in my life, too numerous to list them all. So, I will end with this "Thank You."

Marlene Grimes Stokes, CEO of Stokes & Associates Training Group, a Strategic Intervention Life Coach who provides guidance to immense personal and professional success to women. Contact Marlene info@marlenestokes.com. www.marlenestokes.com.

May 3

Gratitude Becomes A Lifestyle

The art of gratitude is such a Powerful energy, and like a caterpillar that turns into a butterfly, once you transform your mind to make it a lifestyle it's impossible for you to go back to the way you were before. Where are you today in life? Are you at Peace? Are you happy? Do you believe that you can have and can BE anything you want to be? Well, I'm here to let you know that you Can and you WILL!

I challenge you to continue expressing gratitude daily and complete the next seven months of this journal. Not only will gratitude become a way of living for you but it will become a lifestyle. Then and only then will you be able to truly manifest the life you desire to have.

I dedicate this chapter to all of the women who are (is) reading this book to let you know that YOU HAVE THE POWER to BE anything that you desire to be. Be grateful and Go Be GREAT!

Shavannah Speaks Moore is an Entrepreneur, Empowerment Speaker & Author who is on a mission to transform the lives of Women Globally by Empowering them to be the Leaders they were destined to be. She believes that EVERYTHING you need is already in YOU...You just have to tap into your Power! Connect at www.shavannahmoore.com

May 4

Dedicated to Ruby Yeh

I am extremely grateful for a recent epiphany! It had to do with how I respond to situations. Here's what happened…I was invited to participate in a new social media platform that would bring me global visibility. I immediately said no, claiming I didn't have time. As the person who invited me talked me through my decision, it became clear that, in my reaction, I had gone to a place where the glass was empty, to a place of lack. This was an incredible realization! Now that I have awareness of my habit of seeing the glass as empty, I can begin to catch myself in the moment, determine if I reacted with it full or empty, and adjust my behavior accordingly.

You, too, can choose to go to this place where the glass is full, where you see with gratitude. To get there, I invite you to begin to view situations with appreciation. Consider whether you see a full glass, and if not, adjust your thinking. Consider gratitude. Blessings.

Carolyn CJ Jones is an Award-winning Author, Speaker, Forgiveness Coach, and a retired Registered Nurse. At fifty-eight, she overcame the anger and bitterness she'd lived with her entire adult life when she discovered forgiveness and gratitude. As a result, she experiences great peace. Connect with CJ at carolyncjjones.com

May 5

In Honor of My Sister, Tara

Happy belated birthday Tara, my sister who is always in my heart. We have our differences and are definitely opposites in many ways. But one thing I know for sure-- we will always love each other. We have shared laughter, tears, heart-warming moments and disappointment together. We will forever be bonded by our life experiences past, present and future. I am grateful for you (and that you really weren't adopted!!). I love you!

Shannon Gaude is a Co-owner of Hayward Gaude Photography Portrait and Design Studio. Connect with Shannon at shannon@haywardgaudephotography.com and www.haywardgaudephotography.com

_____

_____

_____

_____

_____

_____

_____

_____

_____

_____

_____

_____

_____

May 6

Sometimes if given the opportunity to have a "do over" some say "Heck No, Never Again". I am grateful that even though I did say that. I did it anyway. This is the date I graduated from college in 1976 and 30 years later graduated again. I barely graduated from college in the 70's and had not considered ever reliving that part of my life again. After serving on a medical mission trip. I wanted to serve more, but it required going back to school. I was scared, afraid to repeat my past experience. Despite my fears, and despite what others said, I forged ahead wanting to become a nurse and open a Wellness Center. Before my graduation, I received an announcement from my Alumna and guess what our 30th Reunion was the same day as my graduation from Nursing School. I decided not to go to our reunion because the second time around I had the honor to wear my Honor Society Scroll as I graduated. **No regrets just gratitude of looking ahead and not back.**

Nancy Brewington, a native of New York City, served 20 years in the US Army, retiring in 1997 and received her second degree in nursing in 2006. Nancy, in her passion for helping others, created Hands N Harmony Wellness Center, Universal City, TX in 2011. Contact Nancy at nancybrewington@massagetherapy.com

May 7

"Being rich/wealthy is being in touch with the fullness of life. When you are open to the present moment, what comes in, is a gratitude for "what is". When you are aligned with the present moment, there is a peace that comes, so it is like you are experiencing life for the first time, when you become present. When you are in a state of gratitude for what is ... that is really what being wealthy means."

~ Eckhart Tolle

What is in your life now which you are grateful for? Write down 20 things, can include people. Go, "write" now.

_____

_____

_____

_____

_____

_____

_____

_____

_____

_____

_____

_____

May 8

I am grateful for the power of Will, GOD's Will. My mom taught me to be strong and become stronger no matter the circumstances. She worked every day cleaning houses so we could have the basic necessities; she taught me to work hard and never stop. Idle people, idle minds. Rinse and repeat the routine to survive every day and every year for the rest of her life. I often went to work with her to clean those big and well-furnished homes. As I dusted and polished those rich people's furnishings, I realized as a nine-year-old girl it was not about work but the opportunities. Opportunity meant "Education, Empowerment, and Think Outside of the BOX"! Every employer she worked for had an education either through experience, formal education or a mix of both and motivation!

This GOD's Will manifesting is what I use when dealing with daily obstacles. I use GOD's Will to guide me and redirect me into a higher plain of thinking and a better path life. GOD will show you the way; therefore less stress and happier, clearer windows of opportunities shall arise.

Estela Kelley was born in Corpus Christi, Texas and lives in Pasadena, Texas with her husband and three beautiful kids. She graduated from Texas A&M University-Corpus Christi and is a Business Owner, Headband Designer, Author and a Blogger at www.estelakelley.com.

May 9

"Let us rise up and be thankful, for if we didn't learn a lot today, at least we learned a little, and if we didn't learn a little, at least we didn't get sick, and if we got sick, at least we didn't die; so, let us all be thankful."

~ Buddha

I chuckled at this one because sometimes we do get caught up in what is not a bad/negative situation or event. Yes, I can say it is a good day if I am not in an accident, sick or dead. Buddha did not mean to be sacrilegious about death; his point is well-intentioned; we can learn to swiftly change the course of our thoughts from going down the vortex of "what is wrong" to the uplifting bright blue sky of "what is right".

What did you learn today? What went right for you, for your family, for your job or school? How was this a "gratitude-filled day?

_____

_____

_____

_____

_____

_____

_____

_____

_____

_____

May 10

"Two kinds of gratitude: The sudden kind we feel for what we take; the larger kind we feel for what we give."

~ Edwin Arlington Robinson

Gratitude is not a one-way street, and only for our self and what we have, it is similar to the saying "love is not love until we give it away". To truly **Live In Gratitude Daily**, we are grateful for what we AND we share gratitude with and for others!!

How have you expressed your Live In Gratitude Daily habit? Who were your thankful for and how did you let them know? Thankful not only if they did something to or for you, but truly thankful if something went very well for them and you were grateful for what they received!!

_____

_____

_____

_____

_____

_____

_____

_____

_____

_____

_____

May 11

"There is a law of gratitude, and it is . . . the natural principle that action and reaction are always equal and in opposite directions. The grateful outreaching of your mind in thankful praise to supreme intelligence is a liberation or expenditure of force. It cannot fail to reach that to which it is addressed, and the reaction is an instantaneous movement toward you."

~ Wally Wattles

Your thoughts create energy and vibration, the more positive energy which is created, the more positive is the reaction. Gratitude is a positive emotion attracting other positive emotions and positive value. Our thoughts become things, so be wise and choose gratitude over hate, blame, shame or discontent. We want to create positive energy and vibrations to attract the same thing!!

What "grateful outreaching" of your mind happened today?

_____

_____

_____

_____

_____

_____

_____

_____

_____

_____

May 12

After four months and five specialists, I was finally given the diagnoses I didn't want to hear. "Mrs. Arnold, I am sorry to tell you this but you have inflammatory breast cancer." and he started to cry. His tears were ones of frustration, as he knew I had been misdiagnosed for months. I told him "Thank you." He was surprised at my reaction, but I told him the reason I was thankful is now we had a place to start.

I have celebrated eight bonus birthdays.

Hope always.

Terry Arnold is a Wife and Mother. Terry's mission with the IBC Foundation is to fund research and to provide proactive education to the general population as well as the medical community regarding Inflammatory Breast Cancer. Connect with Terry at www.theibcnetwork.org.

May 13

I struggled with body image issues as a young adult. It started in 6th grade when a friend told me I looked fat in a swimsuit. I was concerned it was true, although I hadn't started getting curves or stretching up yet.

When I was diagnosed with Crohn's Disease in my 20's, I thought, "See? I AM flawed." I was self-conscious, embarrassed, and worried everyone else noticed when my belly was bloated and distended. After years of feeling ashamed of my body, it took a hospitalization to realize that my body was doing everything possible to keep me alive. My heart beats multiple times a day. My lungs breathe. My fingers hold many things. My gut is my intuitive radar. In that hospital bed, I became grateful for my body.

Have you considered everything your body does for you day to day? Take a few minutes to list the ways you're grateful for your body.

Holly Wade *is a Healthy Lifestyle Coach with over two decades of experience in Fitness & Wellness. Through her personal struggles, she knows the toll stress takes on the entire Being. She helps women reduce stress and live vibrantly. Connect with Holly at* holly@hollywadewellness.com

May 14

"Cultivate the habit of being grateful for every good thing that comes to you, and to give thanks continuously. And because all things have contributed to your advancement, you should include all things in your gratitude."

~ Ralph Waldo Emerson

Everything which has happened, everything we have achieved, earned received or been given has brought us to today. We are alive; each day is a new day to move forward, to live then life we truly want. For this be grateful, the past is now behind us, our history and we have today and the future to concentrate on and to make better than the past. Gratitude is what can make our life better.

What was contributed to your advancement, even if your advancement is not what you would like it to be right now? The fact you are alive, reading and writing in this journal means you believe in yourself and are ready for the blessings of today and the tomorrows to come.

_____

_____

_____

_____

_____

_____

_____

_____

_____

_____

_____

_____

May 15

"The highest tribute to the dead is not grief but gratitude."

~ Thornton Wilder

Being in gratitude and thankfulness after the death of a loved one is not the traditional thinking. My father passed away suddenly May 26, 2015. I was very thankful my brother and his family were geographically close to my mom and could be there shortly after his death. As I was flying, we would touch base, and both my brother and mom stated they were talking and remembering dad, laughing at times through the tears, being grateful for all he gave us and being part of our life. Definitely there was sadness, and there still is today; our main focus has been on how grateful we are for him. That has helped us not to be stuck in grief, remembering my dad in gratitude, joy, and laughter, as he wants us to do.

Take a moment and think about someone close to you, who you have lost, what are you grateful about regarding having them in your life?

_____

_____

_____

_____

_____

_____

_____

_____

_____

_____

_____

May 16

"The world is 3 days: As for yesterday, it has vanished along with all that was in it. As for tomorrow, you may never see it. As for today, it is yours, so work on it."

~ Hasan of Basra

"As for today, it is yours, so work on it." Yes, that is the intention of this journal, every day we "so work on it."

What did you do today to "so work on" your gratitude? List 5-10 actions, behaviors, thoughts which were part of your gratitude work today.

_____

_____

_____

_____

_____

_____

_____

_____

_____

_____

_____

_____

_____

_____

May 17

"Thank you' is the best prayer that anyone could say. I say that one a lot. Thank you expresses extreme gratitude, humility, understanding."

~ Alice Walker

How often do you say "thank you"? I was taught to say "thank you" for gestures of kindness, someone holding the door for me, a waiter bringing me a glass of water; for receiving pretty much anything. I realize though it was not a habit for saying "thank you" to waking up; "thank you" for the sun; "thank you" for the rain; I was not saying "thank you" to numerous things which I was grateful for!!   There are always opportunities, big and small to say "thank you".

What did you or what can you say "thank you" for today?

_____

_____

_____

_____

_____

_____

_____

_____

_____

_____

_____

_____

May 18

Today I am grateful to be alive and for each of the blessings that the Lord has provided. I am honored and humbled to be a part of this world and continue to pray to do His (the Lord's) will. Psalm 119:73-74: Your hands made me and formed me; give me understanding to learn your commands. May those who fear rejoice when they see me, for I have put my hope in your word. (NIV) It has been quite the journey of life, yet each experience has made me a stronger person and taught me to keep the faith. Philippians 4:13 I can do everything through Him (the Lord) who gives me strength. (NIV)

What blessings are you most grateful for?

DeLyla Haunschild is a Mother to two and a College Graduate. DeLyla's faith is the one constant that remains throughout her life; she knows she has so many blessings to be grateful and thankful to the Lord for experiencing. Follow DeLyla at www.facebook.com/DeLylaHaunschild or email at DeLyla.Global.247@gmail.com.

_____

_____

_____

_____

_____

_____

_____

_____

_____

_____

_____

_____

May 19

"Gratitude shifts your focus from what your life lacks to the abundance that is already present. In addition, behavioral and psychological research has shown that giving thanks makes people happier and more resilient, it strengthens relationships, it improves health, and it reduces stress. Gratitude will change your life for the better."

~ Marilesa Fabrega

Gratitude is a thought which produces an emotion, with this journal we are creating a habit of gratitude since research shows it is a very positive aspect of our lives.

What are your gratitude thoughts? How many times a day do you find yourself being grateful?

_____

_____

_____

_____

_____

_____

_____

_____

_____

_____

_____

_____

_____

May 20

"Feeling gratitude and not expressing it is like wrapping a present and not giving it."

~ William Arthur Ward

The question came to mind regarding this quote, if we do not express or share our gratitude is it gratitude? The deep, significant, sincere emotion which can bring us abundance, joy, and love? Even if a person we are grateful for cannot hear us, say it out loud, text, email, send a letter. If the person is no longer with us, still share, make the thought and emotion "real".

Have you been grateful or thankful today and did not make it "real" by expressing it? If so write it down now, see the words on paper, feel the gratitude and thankfulness, deep within you.

_____

_____

_____

_____

_____

_____

_____

_____

_____

_____

_____

_____

May 21

"Enough' is a feast."

~Buddhist proverb

Often we are taught the concept of lack, which there is not enough. In most countries, there is more than enough, and basic necessities are available. We often want more; we see others with more; we do not see the gratitude in what we do have. This does not mean we cannot be open to receiving more; it means to be grateful for what we do have, share our gratitude in that and gratitude for more to come.

What do you have which is "enough"? What are you grateful for today?

_____

_____

_____

_____

_____

_____

_____

_____

_____

_____

_____

_____

_____

May 22

There are countless books and articles about gratitude, which has the power to shift negative to positive mindsets. There was a time when my life and body fell apart; I was in the depths of despair. While at this crossroads I realized that I had to take control, look at the truth of my life and focus on what was good versus the pain. One of my spiritual teachers, Abraham-Hicks, gave me a revelation; there is only One River of Life, not a good or a bad one….just ONE! I had a choice to float on the river of life or continue to fight against the current. All I had to do was change my point of awareness. I would ask myself often in a day, "With what is causing my pain to be true, am I OK right now? The answer was always "YES". From there I asked myself, "What is good right now?" Even if I could only find one thing good, I locked onto it with every part of my mind, body, and spirit. Then something wonderful started happening; people showed up to help me, financial gifts were given to me, and my physical pain diminished. I was able to see more good around me and my gratitude expanded so much that I noticed something I hadn't experienced in years, maybe my whole adult life…Inner Peace.

Sharlene Trumet LMT, CWC, CLC, has 22 years of assisting people with their physical, emotional and spiritual well-being. Connect with Sharlene at www.livnbetter4ever.com.

May 23

"Enjoy the little things, for one day you may look back and realize they were the big things."

~Robert Brault

How often do we realize we miss someone or something and realize we did not truly express what we felt, how grateful we were for them and how much we appreciated them. It wasn't that we were given a lot of money or the things were expensive, it was time, fun or comfort we received, and possibly/probably took for granted.

Today, what are the "little things" which you are grateful, what is everything you are grateful for today?

_____

_____

_____

_____

_____

_____

_____

_____

_____

_____

_____

_____

May 24

"As we express our gratitude, we must never forget that the highest appreciation is not to utter words but to live by them."

~ John F. Kennedy

Live In Gratitude Daily includes our thoughts, emotions, and actions of gratitude. We show our gratitude through our kindness, our considerations, our living gratefully.

How are you giving in gratitude to others as you are also grateful and open to receiving in gratitude? Describe what Live In Gratitude Daily is for you. Once you have written this down, re-read it and see if there is anything else you can do, to truly live in gratitude.

May 25

Today, I am grateful for higher education. It has taught me to persevere through challenging times, how to think on my own, work with diverse backgrounds, be strong and independentt and to stay the course until your goal and/or dream becomes a reality. Also, to appreciate the friendships that I gained throughout life. These experiences and individuals have made an impact in my life.

What educational experience and friendship are you grateful for?

DeLyla Haunschild is a Mother to two and a College Graduate. DeLyla's faith is the one constant that remains throughout her life; she knows she has so many blessings to be grateful and thankful to the Lord for experiencing. Follow DeLyla at www.facebook.com/DeLylaHaunschild or email at DeLyla.Global.247@gmail.com.

_____

_____

_____

_____

_____

_____

_____

_____

_____

_____

_____

_____

May 26

The GEMINI was born yet too early on this day; I am grateful to be alive and filled with life! Remember that you can conquer anything!

You hold the power of YOU, and all the keys to your dreams!

Michael Prokopiw is a Senior in High School and enjoys all sports, gaming, and life in general.

_____

_____

_____

_____

_____

_____

_____

_____

_____

_____

_____

_____

_____

_____

_____

_____

May 27

Take a moment, be still and just be. Many of us are moving so fast that we are not taking in the moment. Pray or meditate each day. Acknowledge gratitude in your life by reflecting on your life's journey…its highs AND lows. Finding gratitude in our low points and acknowledging what we have overcome deserves a great deal of recognition.

Spread your gratitude, daily.

Randomly call someone you know just to say, "Thank you" or "I'm thinking of you." You could make someone's day with this small gesture. Everyone wants to feel appreciated.

Crystal Offutt, MBA, is a seasoned, dynamic Interactive Media Developer and Real Estate Broker Associate. She began her career as an entrepreneur at a very young age. On a personal note, she has a wild fascination for active volcanoes! **Connect with Crystal** *at* www.SmithKingMedia.com.

_____

_____

_____

_____

_____

_____

_____

_____

_____

_____

_____

_____

May 28

*"Reflect upon your present blessings, of which every man has plenty;
not on your past misfortunes, of which all men have some."*

~ Charles Dickens

We all make mistakes; hopefully we recognize them, learn from them and do not repeat them again. Hopefully, we are not holding another person's mistake against them. To be in gratitude, we focus on the good, the positive of ourselves and others.

What are the blessings you can focus on today of yourself and those around you?
What do you notice changes in you when you focus on blessings and not "wrongs"?

_____

_____

_____

_____

_____

_____

_____

_____

_____

_____

_____

_____

May 29

"If a fellow isn't thankful for what he's got, he isn't likely to be thankful for what he's going to get."

~ Frank A. Clark

Have you ever said or thought "if only…."? Yes, if only I had a better car, I was thinner, I was married, if I wasn't married, if I had a different job; "if only….". I am not ever thinking "if only" created anything in my life. It is not action-oriented; it is definitely "in lack thinking". If we are truly grateful for today, whatever it is we have, we will be grateful and probably work for what we will receive in the future. We do receive through our work, working with a closed, lack mind or working with an open receiving mind, is the difference.

What are you thankful for today and how did you express it?

_____

_____

_____

_____

_____

_____

_____

_____

_____

_____

_____

_____

May 30

Note to self!

Our lives are built by memories, trials, errors, ups and down, doubt, happiness, love, tenderness, empathy and many, many more experiences and facts. I have grown to understand that I "do not stand alone". I choose not to carry my pain and fear a moment longer, but surrender them to the Lord our God, for He and only He can heal my pain and show me love. My biggest battle has been my relationship with food; I have chosen sweets as my comfort and rescue. It is now... that I understand, My soul belongs to God as He has made me in His likeness, My body I get to borrow for as long as I live. I can finally see; my body is His temple, and as such I will respect, love, and take care of it.

John 14:27 Peace I leave with you; my peace I give to you. I do not give to you as the world gives. Do not let your hearts be troubled; do not be afraid.

Claudia Nava *is a Wife and Mother of two children who loves to have fun and laugh!! She owns two businesses, Claudia Cleaning Services and a direct sales team with Stream. Connect with Claudia at yoko4you.mystream.com.*

May 31

In Dedication to My Dad (Tom Bennett)

Practicing the art of being (embodiment) while doing (empowered action). One divine morning in Mexico, I was standing in tree pose; the ocean waves were rolling towards me, crashing just feet away. As I softened my gaze out over the ocean, there was this perfect moment of deep calm. Everything slowed down; the next wave felt like it stood in an extended pause as a beautiful pelican was gliding by. Time stopped. I was in perfect alignment, standing in full power, anchored and supported by the sand. I embodied the full experience of delight "the light" right through to my core. I let go of judgments and perceptions, allowing myself to simply observe. A whole new experience and view showed up, I saw the world through a new lens and created space for magic to come in. I've taken this experience into my everyday life. When I give myself permission to slow down, soften my gaze and see through a new lens, my empowered next step effortlessly shows up, and abundant evidence follows. Will you give yourself permission today?

Dixie Bennett is on a mission to educate and empower 1 Million women who are healers and leaders to overcome pain and emotional blocks so they are freed to make their impact in the world and create joyful abundance while transforming lives. Connect with Dixie at www.stillpointbodyworks.ca

---

"Gratitude begins at home; with our body, mind, and soul."

~ *Denise Joy Thompson*

"Life is unpredictable, what can be constant is your perspective. Choose gratitude as the foundation of your perspective."

~ Denise Joy Thompson

June

June 1

Gratitude means to be fully present and conscious of our surroundings. To live a healthier, happier and wealthier life, a daily practice of gratitude will place you on that path.

These are five simple, but effective techniques that you can use daily to optimize your life and develop an attitude of gratitude.

1) **Count your blessings**. One-by-one, write down what you're thankful for in life.
2) **Be Intentional**- Gratitude starts with you, and it takes practice. It takes time, patience and most of all, consistency. So, don't give up!
3) **Reposition Your Mindset**- You may not control every event that takes place in the day, but what you do control is how you respond to them.
4) **Share a Touch of Gratitude**- "Thank you" is one of the most powerful and engaging words we can say.
5) **Be Accountable**- Find like-minded individuals that practice gratitude. Connect and share your personal development along the way. You could event make it more interesting with a group by having a gratitude challenge…And hashtag it! #GratitudeChallenge

Chanette Sparks is an American Business Professional, Writer, Small Business Trainer, Digital Media Host and Philanthropic Leader in her industry. She believes by helping individuals position themselves for success, communities will gain leaders. Contact Chanette at Pr@initialsbyjake.com.

_____

_____

_____

_____

_____

_____

_____

_____

_____

_____

June 2

"If you want to turn your life around, try thankfulness.
It will change your life mightily."

~ Gerald Good

The title of this journal, **Live In Gratitude Daily**, **The KEY to abundance, joy and love**, is intended to help and support you to not just try, but to live in thankfulness/gratitude. A lifestyle change takes practice and consistency; this is a lifestyle change, it is a behavioral change which will result in a life you have wanted but wasn't sure how to achieve it. This is one of the simplest changes to make, we learn it, do it and live it.

How do you remember to practice and live in gratitude? Besides this journal, what are "reminders" for you to be grateful? One idea is to place a notecard on the bathroom mirror, even if it has the simplest of messages, **Live In Gratitude Daily**, which you will see every day; or "I am grateful I am here today".

What are your reminders, what are you doing to practice gratitude every day?

_____

_____

_____

_____

_____

_____

_____

_____

_____

_____

_____

_____

June 3

"The world has enough beautiful mountains and meadows, spectacular skies and serene lakes. It has enough lush forests, flowered fields, and sandy beaches. It has plenty of stars and the promise of a new sunrise and sunset every day. What the world needs more of is people to appreciate and enjoy it."

~ Michael Josephson

What are you grateful for regarding where you live? Your home, your city, your state your country? How are you showing your appreciation?

_____

_____

_____

_____

_____

_____

_____

_____

_____

_____

_____

_____

_____

_____

June 4

"Gratitude is a currency that we can mint for ourselves, and spend without fear of bankruptcy."

~ Fred De Witt Van Amburgh

We create our gratitude, the amount which is limitless. Creating gratitude, though it grows with consistency, requires little effort.

How are you growing your limitless amount of gratitude? What have you found is the most rewarding part of creating gratitude?

_____

_____

_____

_____

_____

_____

_____

_____

_____

_____

_____

_____

_____

June 5

In Dedication to My Girls that I am Forever Grateful For

Even in the toughest times, we can normally find at least one thing to be thankful for to pull us through if we try hard enough. It is more challenging to dig deep to find everlasting gratitude that will make the difference in our life. Being grateful for the good, the bad, and especially the ugly in life is what will lead to true abundance in life. That is the gratitude that will open your heart and your mind to positivity. God will never give us more if we are not thankful for what we already have.

I challenge you to dig deep and find 30 things that you are grateful for and why. It is those things that will align you with the deepest gratitude and show you the way through the darkest days that you will face.

Living a life of profound gratitude will lead to a fuller life of abundance.

LeaAnn Fuller is a Women's Empowerment and Fuller Life Coach, Best Selling Author, and Speaker. She is the founder/CEO of Fuller Life, LLC and Adopt-A-Mom program. LeaAnn's passion is to empower women to live their Fuller Life. Connect with LeaAnn at www.lovingyourfullerlife.com.

June 6

I Live in Gratitude in Memory of My Father

My father was a man of faith who taught me the importance of God, faith, and religion. A man who dedicated his life to providing for his children, although we could not understand why much of the foods was grown and raised by him. As we grew older, we realized we had a lot to be grateful for, the many fruit trees we had access to; peaches, pears, plums and many other fruits because many of our friends and cousins were not as fortune as we were. It was my father who taught me the meaning of gratitude (to be thankful) to always be thankful for the things we had and for the things we do not have because they have been things we do not need. I am grateful that he taught me the importance of education and hard work.

Marcel Proust states, "Let us be grateful to the people who make us happy; they are the charming gardeners who make our souls blossom." I agree.

Geraldine Taylor is a Health and Wellness Director at a senior living facility and is the Deputy Executive Director for ImpactSM Charity Inc.: a family owned 501(c3). She is an Organo Gold Independent Distributor. Contact Geraldine at nitro2221@gmail.com.

June 7

"He is a wise man who does not grieve for the things which he has not, but rejoices for those which he has."

~ Epictetus

Focus on the positive which will multiply, focus on the negative and that will multiply. Which one do we want more?

What did you experience today which you can rejoice in? What went right, what and who are you grateful for?

June 8

"At times, our own light goes out and is rekindled by a spark from another person. Each of us has cause to think with deep gratitude of those who have lighted the flame within us."

~ Albert Schweitzer

Who are you grateful for who has lighted the flame within you? When your light was going out, who rekindled it? How did you express your gratitude to them?

_____

_____

_____

_____

_____

_____

_____

_____

_____

_____

_____

_____

_____

_____

June 9

"The deepest craving of human nature is the need to be appreciated."

~ William James

Appreciation, love, gratitude, caring, and tending to are the essence of growth.

How are you expressing and showing appreciation and gratitude for your family? For your co-workers? For you employees? For anyone around you?

_____

_____

_____

_____

_____

_____

_____

_____

_____

_____

_____

_____

_____

_____

June 10

"The way to develop the best that is in a person is by appreciation and encouragement."

~ Charles Schwab

Why do we have so many award systems, we have them in school, sports, and the workplace. Whether they are truly created in a way which works, the idea is to show appreciation with the result of the person feels good and does better!

How do you show appreciation(gratitude) and encouragement to those around you? Are there ways you can do more?

_____

_____

_____

_____

_____

_____

_____

_____

_____

_____

_____

_____

_____

_____

_____

June 11

In Honor of Vulnerability and Love: Open your heart and contemplate how your light can make a difference in the world.

To see the love in your eyes catapulted me into a space of my own growth that I thought I had conquered. I looked in your eyes and was challenged to confront my heart and where I could give more, help more and touch my own heart while being so compassionate to what the group as a whole was facing. To be called home by the Goddess of Pele has softened my heart to where I see how I fit in as a teacher, mentor, trailblazer and most importantly a lover of life and everyone I touch around me. I am drawing to me astounding people I never dreamed possible and the other night with a person who paid me the highest compliment ever. It doesn't matter who it was, but the words "I have been reading what you have been writing to me, and to be honest I really wanted to see if you were the real deal and you really are.". I bowed my head in humility and silently drew all of your energy and love in. My response was short and life continued. **Simple moments like this is when I pause and give thanks to grace.**

Laura Goodman The Shameless Warrior(tm) is the embodiment of reverent authentic love. Her mission is to lend her voice to Warriors of abuse who have not found theirs. Laura is an Author, Mentor, Warrior, Teacher, Speaker, and Advocate. She is here to serve humanity and loves with an open heart, fully and completely. Connect with Laura at www.facebook.com/pg/shamelesswarrior.

_____

_____

_____

_____

_____

_____

_____

_____

_____

June 12

"Be thankful for what you have; you'll end up having more. If you concentrate on what you don't have, you will never, ever have enough."

~ Oprah Winfrey

Write down everything you can think which supports you today?
(Do not limit your thinking, see if you can identify 20 things you have and then say thank you to each one).

_____

_____

_____

_____

_____

_____

_____

_____

_____

_____

_____

_____

_____

_____

_____

_____

June 13

"Gratitude is not only the greatest of virtues, but the parent of all the others."

~ Cicero

Gratitude is the "parent of them all". Yes, Gratitude is the KEY to abundance, joy, and love. This has been known for hundreds of years, though just now we are concentrating on it.

How did you practice gratitude today? How did it make you feel?

_____

_____

_____

_____

_____

_____

_____

_____

_____

_____

_____

_____

_____

_____

_____

_____

June 14

I think it is my basic approach to life the inherently, intuitively, and innately invites Gratitude on a daily basis. It is a basic law of physics that every action necessarily produces a reaction, my approach to life is to be thankful for every little thing and take nothing for granted.

What strategies did you implement to create/have Gratitude (on a daily basis)?

Jeanette B. Marco is Executive Director at MarcoArt New York, is a Get Reel TV Show Host, is Editor in Chief of En' Route Middle East and Cachet Travels USA. Connect with Jeanette at www.itsabeautifullife.us.

_____

_____

_____

_____

_____

_____

_____

_____

_____

_____

_____

_____

_____

_____

_____

_____

June 15

"Silent gratitude isn't very much to anyone."

~Gertrude Stein

Do we truly accept the concept of gratitude if we are not expressing it, sharing it, or verbalizing it?

How are you expressing it, sharing it, or verbalizing it? When you do, what is the response to the people who are receiving, being given your gratitude?

_____

_____

_____

_____

_____

_____

_____

_____

_____

_____

_____

_____

_____

_____

June 16

"Thankfulness is the beginning of gratitude. Gratitude is the completion of thankfulness. Thankfulness may consist merely of words. Gratitude is shown in acts."

~ Henri Frederic Amiel

Gratitude encompasses several other concepts, that of thankfulness, giving, receiving, openness. Gratitude is a way of being including our thoughts, emotions, and actions.

How are you truly living in gratitude? What are your thoughts, emotions, and actions which support your gratitude?

_____

_____

_____

_____

_____

_____

_____

_____

_____

_____

_____

_____

_____

June 17

Today's her birthday. I knew she would be different before she was even born; knew she was meant to bring some change into our lives. I just had no idea it would be from a heroin addiction. For years I participated in my daughter's heroin addiction dancing from victim to bully to rescuer and back again; feeling heartache, anger, guilt, denial, numbness, and hopelessness to hopefulness and more. Today I only feel **LOVE, GRATITUDE,** and **HOPE**. With every fiber of my being, I am deeply grateful that she chose me to be her mom. I am grateful to be a sacred witness to her soul's journey in this life. I am grateful to this drug and this addiction for showing me depths of my soul I might never have known and so many more things. The gratitude is sweet and heals the heartache. She still struggles to find her way back. I know she will, one way or another. Meanwhile, I'll hold the light for her until she discovers her own and I'm eternally grateful for the gift of the addiction and the beauty her soul has shown to me. Love and Gratitude can heal all things.

Joy Brugh is a Life Transitions Coach, Shaman and Energy Healer specializing in empowering women through life's challenges and helping them to transform using a unique combination of modern life coaching, energetic and shamanic healing along with crystalline activations. Visit her at www.joybrugh.com or joy@joybrugh.com

---

June 18

Today is my birthday, and I am grateful for many things, my partner and my wonderful life among them. Today, though, I am grateful to have been born the oldest of four girls. I am most grateful for the close relationships I have with each of my sisters.

As sisters, we share the experiences we had growing up, most importantly the gift of laughter. When we get together, it isn't long before one of them says something that makes me laugh uncontrollably. Such is their gift to me!

Let me share a story of my sisters' generosity. My partner and I decided to get married in October 2008. It wasn't the best time; the recession left me and my business suffering financially, but we decided to do a bare-bones wedding anyway. When my sisters learned of our plans, they organized a beautiful reception for us at a restaurant in Boston and **PAID FOR IT**, making the day extra special. I love my sisters. I know they will be there for me and I for them!

Denise M. D'Amour is a Lawyer, Entrepreneur, and former Bicycle Shop Owner. She recently was certified as a Passion Test Facilitator where she helps people discover and live their passion. Denise is committed to a daily gratitude and meditation practice. Contact Denise at <u>denisedamour@gmail.com</u>*.*

June 19

"You cannot do a kindness too soon because you never know how soon it will be too late."

~ Ralph Waldo Emerson

Don't delay in creating gratitude in your life and as part of that gratitude being kind and showing kindness. How often have we thought we are going to call, talk, see a person, and then we heard they have died? Now it is too late.

Who do you want to be grateful for and show kindness to, even if only a phone call or text? An in-person visit is best, though are other ways to show kindness also.

_____

_____

_____

_____

_____

_____

_____

_____

_____

_____

_____

_____

_____

June 20

"When I started counting my blessings, my whole life turned around."

~ Willie Nelson

Willie Nelson, one of the all-time country legends, he is even saying what we know to be true, though we might not yet be fully livening this truth.

Today is another great day to realize and think about our blessings.

How has today been a blessing to you? Who and what are you grateful for?

_____

_____

_____

_____

_____

_____

_____

_____

_____

_____

_____

_____

_____

_____

June 21

My second attempt at holy matrimony. After a brief 'starter marriage' that was rather toxic, I spent the first three years after that divorce healing; making very cautious decisions with regards to men. Frankly, a relationship was not my priority. It was only after my current husband's attempt at playing cupid for me, failed, that the most cherished friendship blossomed! The catch? I lived in Northern Virginia – and he lived in San Antonio Texas. The crux of the matter is that *both* of us were entering into a second attempt, a major life decision considering I'd have "bonus" kids, and very, very little history. We are not perfect people; therefore, we don't have a perfect marriage. Yet in spite of statistics and personal opinions about our decision to marry – we've thrived! We celebrate 14 years together in 2107. My marriage has taught me patience, forgiveness and most importantly love…when you least expect it.

"I wasn't born in Texas, but I got here as fast as I could"…and made it my HOME.

Angela Lee graduated from James Madison University ('94), has 20 years working in the IT industry, currently works in the insurance industry and is a Rodan and Fields skincare consultant. Angela is a cancer survivor who advocates for others as a Cancer Action Network ambassador volunteer. Follow Angela at www.facebook.com/angelaglee03

_____

_____

_____

_____

_____

_____

_____

_____

_____

_____

_____

June 22

"It is impossible to feel grateful and depressed in the same moment."

~ Naomi Williams

Research shows having a positive mindset and changing one's thoughts has a significant effect on a person's moods and emotions. Gratitude is one way to change our mindset. (This is not saying for those who are clinically depressed therapy is not necessary).

How can you feel or how did you feel grateful today?

_____

_____

_____

_____

_____

_____

_____

_____

_____

_____

_____

_____

_____

_____

June 23

"Things turn out best for people who make the best of the way things turn out."

~ John Wooden

Is the glass half full or half empty? I say the glass is always full, if only with air, which is a necessity of life, so we do not ever want to have the glass completely empty. Also, the glass can always be refilled!!

We are not truly ever empty either; we can "refill" ourselves by having a different perspective, being grateful for something, anything when life seems to be overwhelming.

What can you always turn to or always be grateful for when you are overwhelmed or thinking of giving up? Who or what is it which "refills" you and gives you energy to keep going and looking forward.

_____

_____

_____

_____

_____

_____

_____

_____

_____

_____

_____

_____

_____

June 24

In Memory of My Father, Photios (Fred) Gotsis

Daddy's Little Girl

Daddy, You raised me to be strong
Daddy, You raised me to be fearless
How did you know life would place obstacles on my path requiring me to call upon the strength you instilled in me?

You said I could do anything I set my mind to
Anything anyone else could do and,
If I chose to, I could do it better.

Daddy, how did you know
There would come a day I would need to believe in myself so intensely to do the work I now love to do?

Somehow, you knew the theme for my life would be 'courageous certitude'
Somehow, you knew you were preparing me to become a strong, confident woman.

Daddy, how did you know the core strength you built in me, little by little over time,
One day would be needed to hold up the confident resolute woman you knew I would become?
Daddy, I wonder if from heaven you now know the depth of gratitude I have for the deep self-belief you instilled in me?

Daddy, I wonder if you know this little girl, now a woman, loves you so!

Vicki Gotsis Ceraso is a Feminine Leader, Ultimate Life Strategist, and Author. Vicki's mission is "Leading women to unveil their greatness to the world and step into their power to become the influence the world is crying out for". Contact Vicki at vickiceraso@gmail.com.

_____

_____

_____

_____

_____

_____

June 25

In Dedication to My Mother, Gloria

I love you mom; this poem is for you!

A mother is someone to shelter and guide us,
To love us, whatever we do,
With a warm understanding and infinite patience,
And wonderful gentleness, too.
How often a mother means swift reassurance
In soothing our small, childish fears,
How tenderly mothers watch over their children
And treasure them all through the years.
The heart of a mother is full of forgiveness
For any mistake, big or small,
And generous always in helping her family
Whose needs she has placed above all.
A mother can utter a word of compassion
And make all our cares fall away,
She can brighten a home with the sound of her laughter
And make life delightful and gay.
A mother possesses incredible wisdom
And wonderful insight and skill-
In each human heart is that one special corner
Which only a mother can fill!
Author: Katherine Nelson Davis

Shannon Gaude *is a Co-owner of Hayward Gaude Photography Portrait and Design Studio. Connect with Shannon at* shannon@haywardgaudephotography.com *and* www.haywardgaudephotography.com.

_____

_____

_____

_____

_____

_____

_____

June 26

"Forget yesterday--it has already forgotten you. Don't sweat tomorrow--you haven't even met. Instead, open your eyes and your heart to a truly precious gift--today."

~ Steve Maraboli

Today is a gift, how are you going to be grateful? Write down ten people, actions or situations for which you can be grateful for today?

_____

_____

_____

_____

_____

_____

_____

_____

_____

_____

_____

_____

_____

_____

June 27

"We should certainly count our blessings, but we should also make our blessings count."

~ Neal A. Maxwell

The way in which we receive and appreciate our blessings is what truly make them blessings.

How do you make your blessings count? How do enjoy them, talk about them, express gratitude for them?

_____

_____

_____

_____

_____

_____

_____

_____

_____

_____

_____

_____

_____

_____

_____

June 28

"In ordinary life, we hardly realize that we receive a great deal more than we give, and that it is only with gratitude that life becomes rich."

~ Dietrich Bonhoeffer

Think about all you have "received" in life. We most often realize we are not grateful: we often take what we receive for granted.

What have you received today which you are grateful for and how did you express your gratefulness? If you weren't able to express it today, how can you express it tomorrow?

_____

_____

_____

_____

_____

_____

_____

_____

_____

_____

_____

_____

_____

_____

_____

June 29

*"The only people with whom you should try to get even
are those who have helped you."*

~ John E. Southard

A great message to live by; do not waste thought and energy on "getting back at" or revenge. You moving forward is the best way to deal with any negativity in our lives.

How are you "getting even" with those who have blessed you or to those whom you are grateful. Expressing your gratitude is the best way to show appreciation.

_____

_____

_____

_____

_____

_____

_____

_____

_____

_____

_____

_____

_____

_____

_____

June 30

"I truly believe we can either see the connections, celebrate them, and express gratitude for our blessings, or we can see life as a string of coincidences that have no meaning or connection. For me, I'm going to believe in miracles, celebrate life, rejoice in the views of eternity, and hope my choices will create a positive ripple effect in the lives of others. This is my choice."

~ Mike Ericksen

What will be or were your choices today regarding gratitude? How did you express, share, or live your gratitude?

"Gratitude has the ability to change the worst of moods; a smile, a nod, a simple "thank you" breaks through the grouchiest, grumpiest moods to create a good day."

~ Denise Joy Thompson

July

July 1

In Memory of My Dad, Roger William Thompson

Words cannot express how much I love my dad. I knew he was proud of me; I knew he supported me, I knew he loved me. I also realize I did not show him or tell him enough how much he meant to me; I could have told him every day. I would visit Dad and Mom several times a year; they would vacation with me and visit me wherever I was living, except Turkey, mom did not want to travel there!! We experienced so much together, the forests in California, cruising the east and the west Caribbean, the Grand Canyon from several views; one time we were passing another "Rim view" and dad wanted to stop, and I refused, my famous "once you saw one rock, you have seen them all" comment has not been forgotten. We even experienced a hurricane together while in the Caribbean. My dad knows today how much I care and how grateful I am, even if not always expressed. I am the person I am today because of my dad. I will be forever grateful.

Denise Joy Thompson is a Wife, Mother of three furbabies, Daughter, Sister, Aunt, a #1 International Best-Selling Author, Coach, Colonel in the Air Force Reserve, a Therapist, and Veteran. She is the host of The Power Of A Woman's Voice TV. Denise's mission is for everyone to have the life they can create. Connect with Denise at thecoachalliance@gmail.com and www.facebook.com/group/LiveInGrattiudeDaily.

_____

_____

_____

_____

_____

_____

_____

_____

_____

_____

July 2

"Appreciation is a wonderful thing. It makes what is excellent in others belong to us as well."

~ Voltaire

One thought about how we co-exist is due to our energy and vibration we all are connected. When we see the good in others we see the good in ourselves; when we see what is negative in others, we are experiencing the negative in ourselves.

How are you focusing on gratitude in and of others, which makes you realize more gratitude about yourself? How is this creating a difference in your life?

_____

_____

_____

_____

_____

_____

_____

_____

_____

_____

_____

_____

_____

July 3

In Dedication to My husband, Jeff

Relationships are very important to the growth and development of a person. Marriage is especially important for it allows us to grow with, and without, the person we married, we need to learn to be part of a couple and also an individual. We are interdependent, not co-dependent. Finding the balance for both individuals is what marriage is about.

"True happiness is to enjoy the present, without anxious dependence upon the future, not to amuse ourselves with either hopes or fears but to rest satisfied with what we have, which is sufficient, for he that is so wants nothing. The greatest blessings of mankind are within us and within our reach. A wise man is content with his lot, whatever it may be, without wishing for what he has not."
~ Seneca

Denise Joy Thompson *is a Wife, Mother of three furbabies, Daughter, Sister, Aunt, #1 International Best-Seller Author, Coach, Colonel in the Air Force Reserve, Speaker, Therapist, and Veteran. Denise's mission is for everyone to have the life they can create. Connect with Denise at* www.facebook.com/group/LiveInGrattiudeDaily *and* thecoachalliance@gmail.com.

July 4

"In the end, though, maybe we must all give up trying to pay back the people in this world who sustain our lives. In the end, maybe it's wiser to surrender before the miraculous scope of human generosity and to just keep saying thank you, forever and sincerely, for as long as we have voices."

~ Elizabeth Gilbert

How are you using your "voice" of gratitude? How many times did you say "thank you" today?

July 5

"Let gratitude be the pillow upon which you kneel to say your nightly prayer. And let faith be the bridge you build to overcome evil and welcome good."

~ Maya Angelou

Add the practice of saying "thank you" for another day right before you close your eyes to sleep. After a few days, remember to journal about what this small additional practice of gratitude does for you?

For your writing today, what conversations or interactions did you have which you are grateful for?

_____

_____

_____

_____

_____

_____

_____

_____

_____

_____

_____

_____

_____

_____

July 6

"You pray in your distress and in your need; would that you might pray also in the fullness of your joy and in your days of abundance."

~ Kahlil Gibran

Prayer, words of thanksgiving and gratitude for all we have and all we have yet to receive can be said every day. The positive energy and vibration will attract what our "soul" knows is good for us to have. I no longer ask for specific "wants", I ask to be blessed with what is right for me; which is not always known until it arrives in my life.

What do you pray or ask for? Is it something specific or for general health, wealth, love? **Write down what you are grateful for having already and in what area of your life would you like more blessings?**

_____

_____

_____

_____

_____

_____

_____

_____

_____

_____

_____

_____

_____

July 7

Dedicated to My Wonderful Son, Kyle

The quest for my life purpose was sometimes so front and center in my spirit but at other times, so far removed. Yet this nagging, this knowing, and desire would always powerfully resurface.

My on-going life was a recurring mess, and for decades I sought the answers that my heart knew must be there. Shame, doubt, fear, insecurity, divorce, addiction, eating disorders and so much more defined me. I KNEW this was out of alignment with who God created me to be. I began asking Him for answers, and in His time, my purpose was defined and crystal clear.

Here's the great news! I am not special...at least, not any more special than you are. If I can find my God-given purpose then you can too. There is a plan for your life; the turmoil and dissatisfaction are your fuel to define it. I now understand that every moment of struggle was the path to my purpose. I sought gratitude in each experience. I thanked God as things happened, "this appears awful, God; I can't wait to see the spectacular thing you are doing because I know it will be good". And gratefully...it is.

Sandy Lee-- Sandy means helper and Lee means healer. It is Sandy's life mission to use her gifts, her purpose and the struggles she has overcome to help you overcome yours. Finding your God-given Confidence IS Success and discovering this is transformational and teaches you to finally fly. Find Sandy at happy@sandyleecoaching.com.

July 8

In Dedication to My Husband

What creates a marriage? I was thinking about that, and the thought of diamonds came to mind. Ever wonder why the tradition was created of diamonds and marriage (as in the wedding rings). What makes a diamond? Diamonds are formed when pure carbon is exposed to very high pressures and temperatures. Then a master jeweler creates shapes and polishes the rough stone to its final gem. Considering how a diamond is created you can see how that can apply to marriage when two people can endure the pressure of jobs, career, financial strain, children, poor health and even loss. Like a diamond having a master jeweler, a good marriage allows God to mold their lives and love is going to be like a piece of coal created to a precious gem like a diamond. I am so grateful I have found my soul mate, my rough coal turned into a fine gem. Through all the rough times and trials of our love, we allowed God to shape and polish not only each of us as individuals, but as a couple creating our lives and marriage to be precious and invaluable.

Nancy Brewington, native of New York City, served 20 years in the US Army, retiring in 1997 and received her second degree in nursing in 2006. Nancy, in her passion for helping others, created Hands N Harmony Wellness Center, Universal City, TX in 2011. Contact Nancy at nancybrewington@massagetherapy.com.

July 9

"One should either be a work of art, or wear a work of art."
~ Oscar Wilde

Have you ever noticed that wearing all black or all white can rob your face of color making you look washed out? I sometimes feel like it can make me feel like my spirit has been robbed of joy too. Color brings me joy and can do the same for you. Easily find ways to add your favorite color into your life each day. It might be on your lips, a small piece of jewelry, a little eyeliner, or maybe even your nail polish. Think about how each color makes you feel when you are surrounded by it. Then decide how you want to feel each day and add the corresponding color to your outfit and watch your FABulousness shine through.

I am grateful for the color _____ because it makes me feel _____.

Allison "FAB" Howell- Social Worker by day, Life Stylist by night teaching women to feel FABulous in Life & Style. Allison combines experience in fashion and psychology to inspire lives to be fun, fresh, and full of FABulous love. www.FABover.com.

_____

_____

_____

_____

_____

_____

_____

_____

_____

_____

_____

July 10

"Gratitude also opens your eyes to the limitless potential of the universe, while dissatisfaction closes your eyes to it."

~ Stephen Richards

With practicing gratitude or at least beginning to practice it, what are you more aware of in your life? What are you more grateful for now than before this awareness?

_____

_____

_____

_____

_____

_____

_____

_____

_____

_____

_____

_____

_____

_____

_____

July 11

EVERYDAY GRATITUDE

I am grateful.

I'm grateful for my parents.

I'm grateful for all the choices I've made – I've either been burned by them, or learned from them

I'm grateful for my husband making most days feel like Valentine's Day, my Birthday or Christmas

I'm grateful for my good health, clean water, a home, and a car

I'm grateful for my family – my longest friendships are with my cousins – and part of my life, for all my life

I'm grateful for the teachers – who taught the engineers, the healers, the tradesmen, and the dreamers

I'm grateful for my girlfriends – ever-present, ever wise, unique, and truly gifts

I'm grateful for pets – they really do bring unconditional love into our lives 365 days a year

I'm grateful for all the children in my life – I love and appreciate their perspective, playfulness and how easily they laugh

I'm grateful I have a commute to complain about – because I have a job

I'm grateful for the few sad days – because I know I've had many more glad days

I am very grateful.

Laurie Vallas delights in observing the patterns between people and events and drawing unconventional associations between the two. She particularly enjoys the challenge of transforming these opportunities into meaningful, influential connections. The pursuit of revealing 'the heartifacts' within everything has become the foundation of Laurie's work. Happy to connect on FB: The Heartifacts, PositiviTEAs or at theheartifacts@gmail.com

July 12

There is no better feeling in this world than love. I am so immensely grateful for the people and experiences in this life that have helped me feel it. It's the late night conversations with my grandparents, the boy in the hallway who I can't help but blush at every time our gaze crosses paths, when the moon comes out and the midnight rain begins, lulling me to sleep to dream dreams that will put a smile on my face the moment I wake, how I will sit on the couch for hours watching the romantic movies I love and will always love, the way I open my favorite book and get lost in the story even though I've already finished it time and time again.

These are the small adventures in my life I wouldn't be the person without. It's why I'm grateful for love.

Caroline Witherspoon is 16 and lives in Washington State. Caroline has always had a passion for writing and aspires to turn that passion into a career.

July 13

In Dedication to Grandmothers

Today I am grateful for Grandmothers. She has been instrumental in shaping my life and becoming the person that I am. I truly thank the Lord for blessing me with such an extraordinary individual and to have had the opportunity to witness such respect, gratitude and appreciation for both faith and sharing it with others. She was a trailblazer, career woman, community leader and made time for others to make them feel and understand that they too are important and dignified. She had such a love of life, and for others that she totally shined through Him (the Lord) in everyday life.

Who are you grateful for that has helped shape your life?

DeLyla Haunschild is a Mother to two and a College Graduate. DeLyla's faith is the one constant that remains throughout her life; she knows she has so many blessings to be grateful and thankful to the Lord for experiencing. Follow DeLyla at www.facebook.com/DeLylaHaunschild or email at DeLyla.Global.247@gmail.com.

July 14

I chose this date because this is the day I was born. I am grateful for my parents who brought me into this world, worked hard and played hard. They gave my sisters and I great memories and a stable foundation to build our lives upon. They were there for us in hard times, and as I've grown older, I am more and more grateful for their understanding and discipline.

My parents were great role models. I grew up in Northern Michigan, and one afternoon there was a tornado warning. This was very rare where we lived so my sisters and I were really scared. The weather got bad quickly, and we headed down to the basement. At that time our basement was unfinished and we huddled to one end. My mom pulled out a paper time clock and started quizzing us on how to read time. This was great because we were distracted from the fear of a tornado and learned to read time. Parenting is the art of distraction.

Kimberly Meyers served 26 years in the Air Force; upon retiring she created her fitness business, Fitness Kinektions. She has 24 years' experience as a Group Fitness Instructor, is a certified Leadership Coach, Personal Trainer and holds an Associates in Kinesiology. Connect with Kimberly at www.fitnesskinektions.com

_____

_____

_____

_____

_____

_____

_____

_____

_____

_____

_____

July 15

On July 15th, 1972 I married a very special man, Les Wiszowaty, and it was all thanks to a friend of my father's. I was at work December 6th, 1971 when I saw Henry on the Concourse of the building where I was working. Henry invited me to dinner, having recently moved away from home and working at my first job since finishing school a free meal is something to be grateful for. Little did I know that night would turn into a romance that has lasted all these years. I thought Henry was taking me to a restaurant for dinner, but it turned out we were going to a farewell party and when Les answered the door, Henry handed him the keys to his car telling Les that he was to drive me home that night. Les did drive me home that night and we have been together ever since. One spontaneous moment allowed this day to happen and because of it my life has been full of spontaneous moments and adventure with my husband, Les.

Janet Wiszowaty is a retired Royal Canadian Mounted Police Dispatcher, Internet Radio Show Host of Worldly Connektions and a Visionary Coach/Mentor who is passionate about helping our First Responders who had a trauma/PTSD and are ready to move forward with their life. Connect with Janet at www.familyconnekt.com.

July 16

"To be grateful is to recognize the Love of God in everything He has given us - and He has given us everything. Every breath we draw is a gift of His love, every moment of existence is a grace, for it brings with it immense graces from Him.
Gratitude therefore takes nothing for granted, is never unresponsive, is constantly awakening to new wonder and to praise of the goodness of God. For the grateful person knows that God is good, not by hearsay but by experience. And that is what makes all the difference."

~ Thomas Merton

God, Spirit, the Universe, our Higher Power, through our faith of good in the world, we are to receive blessings for which we are grateful. If we do not acknowledge and accept the blessings, then it is difficult to receive more.

What are the blessing and gifts in your life, which you may have previously overlooked? How open are you to receiving blessings and gifts? How are open are you to expressing gratefulness for all you have received?

_____

_____

_____

_____

_____

_____

_____

July 17

Dedicated to My Amazing Daughter, Kirstie

Confidence; how in the world could I get gut level, unshakeable, unmistakable confidence? How can you? I was given an assignment by a coach that I was upset about. I thought, "I can't do this". Each day for two weeks I needed to find something I loved about myself, and I was not allowed to repeat. Torture!

I discovered through my willingness, so many things I could love about myself. Gratefully, I continued this work far beyond our two-week agreement. I even began to look forward to it. My gratitude is for the willingness to do whatever I need to so I can live my authentic life. I'm grateful that looking within changed how I see myself.

My suggestion is to be willing to look where you don't want to look. Seek with gratitude and thank God for showing you exactly how He sees and designed you. Find gratitude in the beauty of you, including your less favorable qualities which give birth to your peace. Having gratitude for this assignment and your uniqueness will change you. YOU are the only you the world will ever have; be confident in being you.

Sandy Lee-- Sandy means helper and Lee means healer. It is Sandy's life mission to use her gifts, her purpose and the struggles she has overcome to help you overcome yours. Finding your God-given Confidence IS Success and discovering this is transformational and teaches you to finally fly. Find Sandy at happy@sandyleecoaching.com.

July 18

I Live in Gratitude to Celebrate the Birthday of My Husband, we have managed to celebrate all of his birthdays together

In 2011, the birthday we celebrated seemed as if it was going to be the last one together. He had a near-life-ending illness. I spent many days and nights sleeping in chairs and on the floor of many rooms at the Veterans Hospital, watching him not eat, losing weight to a weight I have never seen. Through the work specialist and nurses at the Audie L Murphy Hospital in San Antonio, Teas I live in gratitude every day. He spent weeks in Rehab, and I am proud and grateful he did a lot to Rehab himself. I am grateful he is much better and living a fairly normal life, he will have one of his two books out in 2017

Maya Angelou said "Let gratitude be the pillow upon which you kneel to say your nightly prayer. And let faith be the bridge you build to overcome evil and welcome good."

Geraldine Taylor is a Health and Wellness Director at a senior living facility and is the Deputy Executive Director for ImpactSM Charity Inc.; a family owned 501(c3). She is also an Organo Gold Independent Distributor. Contact Geraldine at nitro2221@gmail.com

July 19

"No one who achieves success does so without the help of others. The wise and confident acknowledge this help with gratitude."

~ Alfred North Whitehead

I know there were many people along my journey supporting me in my accomplishments and achievements. We do not always recognize them for their help as it is occurring, nor do we always realize who it is who did help us.

Who are the unacknowledged people who have helped throughout your life? Name them and lift up words of gratitude to them. If possible, reach out to them and thank them now.

_____

_____

_____

_____

_____

_____

_____

_____

_____

_____

_____

_____

_____

_____

July 20

"Gratitude and attitude are not challenges; they are choices."

~ Robert Braathe

How are you getting your "attitude of gratitude on"? What are you doing on a daily basis to build your Live In Gratitude Daily habit?

_____

_____

_____

_____

_____

_____

_____

_____

_____

_____

_____

_____

_____

_____

July 21

In Memory of The Best Dad in The World, Doug Liss, 1928-2016; Thanks Dad for All you Taught Me.

My Dad was the kindest man I knew. What did I learn from him that makes me so grateful? He always said, "Just because something is different doesn't mean it is wrong. It means it is different." He was military, and we moved all over the world. People do things differently. He wanted us to learn to evaluate and not judge based on our past experiences, traditions, and habits. It might be right, or it might be wrong. But it is never wrong simply because it is different! The gift of that attitude from Dad has allowed me the freedom to explore many cultures and ideas. I have a belief that each person and each issue is worth examining for value. It would be sad to miss something important or fun just because it was a strange way of approaching it. If you find yourself disagreeing, though, feel grateful because contrast brings clarity for you for your position! Is there a lesson you learned from a parent or teacher that makes you grateful?

Wendy Stout, Ph.D. was a stay at home mom of three who went back to school at age 50 to earn degrees in Natural Healing, including a Ph.D. She leads workshops in EFT (Emotional Freedom Techniques) and the Law of Attraction. Connect with Wendy at https://sway.com/s/OTOBj3K12vZYGy0K/embed.

July 22

Today is my Freedom Day. I started 2011 with a dull existence and a dream: I wanted to quit my job and run my own business. At the time, I didn't even have a business, but I didn't let that stop me. I hired a coach and put everything I had into making it happen. Six months later, I quit my job. July 22, 2011, was my last day working for someone else.

Since then, I'm grateful for the freedom to build my destiny. I never do anything dull anymore. I don't commute, and I never attend teleconferences. I don't even wear pants. I get to choose what I work on and what my life looks like. As I learn and grow, it keeps getting better and better.

I share this story to point out that gratitude doesn't have to stop with appreciating what we have. We can also create our own reasons for gratitude. What could you build that would set you up to be happy and grateful for years to come?

Cara Stein, Ph.D. *believes everyone deserves to be happy. Cara's mission is to help you build your dream life—one simple, concrete step at a time. Learn more and get your free Practical Dreams Kit at* http://17000-days.com/gratitude.

_____

_____

_____

_____

_____

_____

_____

_____

_____

_____

July 23

"No man has ever lived that had enough of children's gratitude or woman's love."

~ William Butler Yeats

Or woman, no one can ever have enough gratitude and love.

How are you showing your gratitude and love? When you do this, how does it make you feel? How are you responding when gratitude and love are given to you?

_____

_____

_____

_____

_____

_____

_____

_____

_____

_____

_____

_____

_____

_____

_____

_____

July 24

Dedicated to My Son, Andrew Pineda; May he always be a light to the world as he is a light to me

As my eyes open each morning, I give Thanks that I've been gifted another day to live.

Throughout the day, as things are unfolding, again, I give Thanks for the moments, people and even when things get difficult because even those are moments that I'm blessed to experience. As I lay my head to rest at the end of the day, I once again do a quick re-cap of the gifts I've experienced and received that day and fall asleep giving Thanks.

I truly believe I am where I am today because of this practice that I have begun in my life. I'm grateful for it **ALL**!

Alma Soul Pineda moved to Maui from Los Angeles in 2015. She embodies the Aloha spirit. A mother of two amazing young men, she was drawn to Maui, to inspire and help others see the beauty in life through Love, Faith, and Trust. She also envisions the world being able to heal holistically. Contact Alma at www.facebook.com/biomatmiraclemaui.

July 25

Every day, I am so thankful for the gift of breath, of life my Creator, God blesses me. This mindset of blessings leaves me with the awareness that every moment is God's time. I have grown over the years and developed some unique core traits. These traits carry me through joys and sorrow, in all aspects of my life. So let's reflect, what core traits we can claim, and lead in all aspects of our lives.

Martha Chua is a transplant to Mississippi from Singapore. Life journey towards light is her life pursuit of purpose, wisdom, and enlightenment to inspire others with her unique life lessons learned and experienced and to be a difference in lives of others. Connect with Martha at lifejourneytowardslight@gmail.com.

July 26

"The smallest act of kindness is worth more than the grandest intention."

~ Oscar Wilde

Intentions do not manifest without attention and action. One of the lessons learned during my Passion Test Facilitator course was "Intention, Attention, No Tension." What we focus on grows, what we do nets results. Act to give and receive.

How are you acting in gratitude? How are you showing thanks to and for others?

July 27

*"Now and then it's good to pause in our pursuit of happiness
and just be happy."*

~ Guillaume Apollinaire

When we spend too much time thinking, preparing, rehearsing, revising, we often to not get anything done. Sometimes we just do it!! No waiting, no procrastinating, no waiting for it to be perfect.

How are you grateful today? Not wishing for something to be different, not wondering what you will receive, just being grateful? What are you grateful for right now?

_____

_____

_____

_____

_____

_____

_____

_____

_____

_____

_____

_____

_____

_____

July 28

"Kindness is the language which the deaf can hear and the blind can see."

~ Mark Twain

Kindness is the universal language.

What acts of kindness did you include in your Live In Gratitude Daily habit?

_____

_____

_____

_____

_____

_____

_____

_____

_____

_____

_____

_____

_____

_____

_____

_____

July 29

In Dedication to My Son

Looking at the significance of this date, well like most parents, the date of their child brings fond memories; for me, it has more of a significant memory. This is the day my son was born. His birth was a happy occasion, and it is so much more; I am so grateful for the person I have become, not only to learn to love my son but to learn to love myself. As a single parent, while serving in the US military miles away from family, friends or any support system during a time that just prior military members were not allowed to be a single parent. I learned to travel on a less-traveled path. It was very difficult, sometimes spending months away and leaving my son with strangers. I had doubts if I was a good parent while serving in the military. One day as I was expressing my doubts as a parent to my son, he looked at me and told me I was the best parent ever, and he is the person he is because of me. I am grateful for my son.

Nancy Brewington, a native of New York City, served 20 years in the US Army, retiring in 1997 and received her second degree in nursing in 2006. Nancy, in her passion for helping others, created Hands N Harmony Wellness Center, Universal City, TX in 2011. Contact Nancy at nancybrewington@massagetherapy.com.

July 30

"Showing gratitude is one of the simplest yet most powerful things humans can do for each other."

~ Randy Pausch

I have heard some people think holding the door is old fashioned or unwarranted. To me, it was a way of someone saying "I appreciate and care about you". It was a way of showing gratitude. It also allowed me to say "thank you" and show gratitude to them.

What are the simple ways you show gratitude, perhaps even without reason?

_____

_____

_____

_____

_____

_____

_____

_____

_____

_____

_____

_____

_____

*"Gratitude builds the foundation, brick by brick, to "house"
abundance, joy and love."*

~ Denise Joy Thompson

August

August 1

After we have seen how other teachers keep their students in check, we are introduced to the unusual John Keating (Robin Williams), the new English teacher who displays ideas and a spirit that deviates sharply from the establishment at Welton. From the start, Keating is a provocative and inspiring educator. During his very first class, Mr. Keating demonstrates he's not just there to convey academic information, but to show the students about life. It was not so much a lesson in English Literature as they stood looking at a glass case of past students, but a dramatic philosophical wake-up call when he recites:

Gather the rosebuds while ye may,
Old Time is still a-flying;
And this same flower that smiles today,
Tomorrow will be dying.

"Why does Robert Herrick write these lines?" he asks.
"Because we are food for worms, lads! Because we're only going to experience a limited number of springs, summers, and falls. And one day, each of you will be fertilizing daffodils."

(Whispering) Carpe Diem! **Carpe Diem--Seize the day. Make your lives extraordinary!**

Jane A. Heron is a Keynote Speaker, a Podcasting Coach, and the Gutsy GURU at www.ThanksAndGrowRich.com

---

August 2

Thank you to my children (Dia, TyDamond, Lakia and Jalin) for believing and pushing me. Thank you to my mom (Zinnie L. Andrews) for always pushing me and not backing down on doing what you feel is best for us all. Thank you daddy (Kenneth Mills) for always being there and for the should've, could've, would've speech that helps push me. Thank you dad (Titus Andrews) for the gift of military service and listening. To my big brother/my Bubba (Damond Andrews) thanks for always standing firm on pushing me never to accept anything but get what I deserve. To my Pastor (Larry J. Thompson)s may God continue to cover you sir, may He continue to speak into your life that you may teach us according to what thus says the Lord, thank you for always praying, and my Tree Mount Temple Church family thank you for embracing my children and me, for allowing God to use each one of you and your gifts.

Jada Andrews is a God-fearing Mother, Daughter, Disabled Veteran & a Business Owner, who's taken the challenges of life and turned them into stepping stones towards greatness. She is the owner of A Mustard Seed, she puts God first and walks in victory. Connect with Jada at www.facebook.com/AMustardSeed75.

August 3

> *"A grateful mind is a great mind which eventually attracts to itself great things."*

~ *Plato*

What are you attracting? What are you receiving from the world around you? When we are living a life of gratitude, there are many things we lose…drama, anger, blame, shame, guilt.

What is different in your life? What have you gained through your gratitude?

_____

_____

_____

_____

_____

_____

_____

_____

_____

_____

_____

_____

_____

August 4

"Gratitude is a quality similar to electricity; it must be produced and discharged and used up in order to exist at all."

~ William Faulkner

How are you using your "electricity" of gratitude? Do you feel the energetic resonance of being grateful? How does this feel to you and what do you enjoy about this feeling?

August 5

Today in this hectic and chaotic world where we need to constantly prove ourself in terms OF competition, we often forget we already have so much in our bag before we ask for more. We often end up comparing our self with others and feel that we fall short of lot of things in our life. This in turn leads to failure and disappointment. The moment we start giving thanks for the smallest things we start feeling confident. The feeling of hopeless and disappointment vanishes. This confidence further pushes us to get more. Being aware and thankful for the smallest deed in our life will never make us feel empty but imbibe a positive spirit to achieve more.

Mansi Parmar was born and raised in India and settled in Canada. Mansi is a Biotechnologist, a Home Maker, and a Crafter. Connect with Mansi at Mansiparmar06@gmail.com.

August 6

"Gratitude is a currency that we can mint for ourselves, and spend without fear of bankruptcy."

~ Fred De Witt Van Amburgh

Gratitude continues to multiply the more we create it, express it, share it, and show it.

How are you creating your "gratitude currency? How have you expressed, shared, or shown your gratitude today?

_____

_____

_____

_____

_____

_____

_____

_____

_____

_____

_____

_____

_____

_____

August 7

"There is no such thing as gratitude unexpressed. If it is unexpressed, it is plain, old-fashioned ingratitude."

~ Robert Brault

Sometimes we just need to see/hear it like it is. When we Live In Gratitude Daily, we show it and people know it. What came to mind was a song I learned in Sunday school, "if you're happy and you know it clap your hands (clap, clap). (Some of you are now singing along, aren't you!!) Often we want to acknowledge and are not sure how, or will it be received the correct way?

The thing about building a gratitude habit is to just do it. Express away, do not shy away from it, others want and need and may not know how to start. You are here, on this journey and what you ae learning, you can share.

How have you expressed your gratitude today? What are some ideas of what you can do tomorrow?

_____

_____

_____

_____

_____

_____

_____

_____

_____

_____

August 8

In Dedication to My Son

My son was born on 8-8-08 and my life has never been the same since. My faith in God strengthens daily as I watch my heart walk around outside my body. I have grown deeper and deeper in my relationship with God so that my faith keeps me sane when I can't be with my son to protect him daily.

Before I had him, I knew I was saved by my faith and lived a fancy and carefree life. After I had him, I focused my eyes on God and continued to keep my eyes and ears on His Words. My son has made me feel complete. I tell him every day that I will love him forever and like him always, and he is my favorite thing in this world. And for that angel being bestowed on me to take care of, love and guide in the ways of the Lord, I am sooooooo thankful.

Jacqi Leyva-Hill is the Founder/Owner of Jacqi's NuFitness Llc & a Minority Partner of the Vegas Stiletto Fitness Llc. Jacqi holds a M.Ed. in Exercise Science, obtained in 1995, and is a Licensed Medical Massage Practitioner and a Patented Inventor. Connect with Jacqi at Jnf-sa.com.

August 9

"Gratitude is an art of painting an adversity into a lovely picture."

~ Kak Sri

Our perspective, internalization and/or personalization is what makes a situation a problem or an opportunity.

How is your gratitude changing how you are "appraising" situations? What is the difference in you how you react, are you now taking more time to figure out your "action" rather than a quick "reaction?

_____

_____

_____

_____

_____

_____

_____

_____

_____

_____

_____

_____

_____

August 10

"To speak gratitude is courteous and pleasant, to enact gratitude is generous and noble, but to live gratitude is to touch Heaven."

~ Johannes Gaertner

In reviewing your gratitude on a daily basis, as much as possible, **what are the changes you see in yourself? What are you doing on a consistent basis to "apply" gratitude in everything you do? Write down not just the "living" of gratitude, look deeper and write down what you feel/see in your heart and mind, look beneath the surface to the inner changes.**

_____

_____

_____

_____

_____

_____

_____

_____

_____

_____

_____

_____

_____

_____

_____

August 11

Ageless Recipe for Creating Gratitude

Gratitude holds many powers. At times it flows abundantly bringing forth joy and contentment. At other times it seems hard to find as the winds of the world take hold. Learning to tap into gratitude's deepest power is found when offering service to another. As we struggle to find the good in the world, we can lose sight of our abundance. Pushing outside of ourselves, placing our focus on how we may help another magically lifts our downtrodden spirit. Thus creating a recipe for gratitude not only for the one receiving help but also for the one willing to offer it. It truly can be magical. Next time you find yourself struggling, find someone you can offer assistance to and watch how your gratitude is renewed.

Laurie Hartley Moore is an entrepreneur at heart with 30 years of experience. She loves people. Laurie loves creating opportunities that help people acquire their dreams, and she love teaching people how to have joy in every aspect of their life. Connect with Laurie at www.ADestinyByDesign.com.

August 12

"Gratitude is the state of mind of thankfulness. As it is cultivated, we experience an increase in our sympathetic joy, our happiness at another's happiness. Just as in the cultivation of compassion, we may feel the pain of others, so we may begin to feel their joy as well. And it doesn't stop there."

~ Stephen Levine

I have noticed on my gratitude journey; I am more emotionally open and aware.

What have you been experiencing emotionally? Do you find yourself more open and vulnerable? Are you experiencing more emotions or feeling more deeply than before? If so, this is to be expected; we are opening up to giving and receiving and with that comes awareness of everything around us.

_____

_____

_____

_____

_____

_____

_____

_____

_____

_____

_____

_____

August 13

"We often take for granted the very things that most deserve our gratitude."

~ Cynthia Ozick

What do you find yourself being in gratitude for now, which in the past seemed commonplace and expected? What do you appreciate more now than before?

_____

_____

_____

_____

_____

_____

_____

_____

_____

_____

_____

_____

_____

_____

August 14

In Honor of Karen and Michael, two people who I love dearly!

When I was struggling to find my way you were honest and gave me the strength to do what I knew in my heart needed to be done. Because of your love, I found the courage to ask for help and lean on my family! You are part of that family even if it is not biologically. There will never be enough words to thank you. Now we are many miles apart, but I miss you every day and carry you in my heart!

I believe that people's paths cross for a reason. Our relationship has a special bond, for this, I am grateful every day!

Shannon Gaude is a Co-owner of Hayward Gaude Photography Portrait and Design Studio. Connect with Shannon at shannon@haywardgaudephotography.com and www.haywardgaudephotography.com.

August 15

Today, I am thankful for new beginnings, my faith, and knowing that change is a great thing. Jeremiah 29:11 For I know the plans I have for you, declares the Lord, plans to prosper you and not to harm you, plans to give you hope and a future. (NIV) The Lord is bigger than all of this, has walked before us, and now is walking alongside us. Walking by faith, not by sight, even though we may not necessarily know all of the intricate details of the future, just knowing that the Lord is here with us every step of the way first and foremost helps to put things in perspective and to be patient to His timing.

What are you grateful for today?

DeLyla Haunschild is a Mother to two and a College Graduate. DeLyla's faith is the one constant that remains throughout her life; she knows she has so many blessings to be grateful and thankful to the Lord for experiencing. Follow DeLyla at www.facebook.com/DeLylaHaunschild or email at DeLyla.Global.247@gmail.com.

August 16

"Gratitude is one of the sweet shortcuts to finding peace of mind and happiness inside. No matter what is going on outside of us, there's always something we could be grateful for."

~ Barry Neil Kaufman

Live In Gratitude Daily: The KEY to abundance, joy, and love. The title says it all.

What are you experiencing more of by living in gratitude? What has changed from before starting this journey? What are you most grateful for?

_____

_____

_____

_____

_____

_____

_____

_____

_____

_____

_____

_____

_____

_____

August 17

"Piglet noticed that even though he had a Very Small Heart, it could hold a rather large amount of Gratitude."

~ A.A. Milne in Winnie-the-Pooh

It does not matter about one's circumstances, skills or talents, all of us have the ability to cultivate gratitude.

How are you cultivating and growing your gratitude? What has helped you and what seems to be more difficult in "living gratitude every day? How are you overcoming the difficulties?

_____

_____

_____

_____

_____

_____

_____

_____

_____

_____

_____

_____

_____

_____

_____

August 18

"Gratitude goes beyond the 'mine' and 'thine' and claims the truth that all of life is a pure gift. In the past I always thought of gratitude as a spontaneous response to the awareness of gifts received, but now I realize that gratitude can also be lived as a discipline. The discipline of gratitude is the explicit effort to acknowledge that all I am and have is given to me as a gift of love, a gift to be celebrated with joy."

~ Henri J.M. Nouwen

This might be one of my favorite quotes. Love, joy, celebration, all is within reach when living in and with gratitude.

How are you seeing the love for yourself increasing with living in gratitude? How much more love and joy do you see in your life? Is this difficult for you to see and feel? If so, what thoughts are in the way? What can you do to change the direction of the thoughts which are not allowing you to fully experience and practice gratitude?

_____

_____

_____

_____

_____

_____

_____

_____

_____

_____

August 19

Dedicated to My Father, James Anthony Day Sr.

When I think about gratitude, I am always reminded of family. I was fortunate enough to have been raised in a family that demonstrated deep love and caring towards each other. Though we encountered difficulties, love was never absent, and we always came back to one another stronger and more loving. My father taught me the importance of never allowing arguments to strip you of the love and gratitude you need to have about family. For many years in my 20's, I often didn't appreciate his advice, because I was angry at someone or hurt. As I have grown older, I understand why he was so adamant that I engrave this advice in my heart every day. It is easy to be swayed by petty arguments, anger, hurt and sadness that others may not meet our expectations. It is vital that you build on the treasures of the heart, be vigilant in expressing your love and support to family members. The more gratitude you feel, the greater your heart expands. So feed the value of gratitude and allow your treasures of the heart to grow stronger and deeper every day.

Jean Day has a Master's degree in Clinical Psychology from Pepperdine University, is a college instructor, for 18 years, and a guest expert on numerous radio shows discussing topics about psychology and wellness. Jean is a Nichiren Buddhist and a member of the Soka-Gakkai USA Buddhist organization. Contact Jean at jeanday319@yahoo.com.

August 20

"Gratitude bestows reverence, allowing us to encounter everyday epiphanies, those transcendent moments of awe that change forever how we experience life and the world."

~ John Milton

There are certain themes which are interwoven within the words of the experts, the writers, the historians, for hundreds of years, there have been "hidden" words of wisdom. You, we, now have the opportunity to take the words of wisdom and to experience all the benefits which gratitude can provide us. This does not cost money or time, it does require effort and thought on the part to incorporate gratitude into our heart, mind and our actions.

How are you incorporating gratitude into your life? What is helping you to remember? Besides this journal are there are books you are reading? Lists, reminders you are creating? If you realize you have forgotten to be grateful or appreciative, do you act on what was forgotten?

August 21

"Gratitude is the moral memory of mankind."

~ Georg Simmel

How is living in and with gratitude changing how you view the world around you? How is it changing your actions and thoughts of right and wrong, how to treat yourself and to treat others? What are you most appreciative of regarding how you interact with others since focusing on gratitude?

_____

_____

_____

_____

_____

_____

_____

_____

_____

_____

_____

_____

_____

_____

_____

August 22

In Dedication to My Parents

Today I am grateful for my parents. They have been an absolute blessing in my life, our family, and continue to make a difference in the lives of others. They have taught me so much about life, how to remain humble, how to love and to understand that with God on our side, anything is possible. 1Corinthians 13:4-7 Love is patient, love is kind. It does not envy; it does not boast, it is not proud. It is not self-seeking, it is not easily angered, it keeps no record of wrongs. Love does not delight in evil but rejoices with the truth. It always protects, always trusts, always hopes, always perseveres. (NIV)

What memory of your parents are you grateful for?

DeLyla Haunschild is a Mother to two and a College Graduate. DeLyla's faith is the one constant that remains throughout her life; she knows she has so many blessings to be grateful and thankful to the Lord for experiencing. Follow DeLyla at www.facebook.com/DeLylaHaunschild or email at DeLyla.Global.247@gmail.com.

August 23

"Gratitude is the sign of noble souls."

~ Aesop

In this context, noble is "taking the high road", when we are living from a heart and mind of gratitude, we move away from anger, blame, pettiness, revenge, and shame. We know to act with the best intentions toward every situation. This does not mean we do not stand up for our self; this means even when we need to do so it is with kindness and acceptance we are interacting with a person who is having their problems, no better or worse than our self, just at a different point in their journey.

How are you acting towards and responding to others when there is a disagreement or a "wrong"? Are you responding differently? Are you more aware of acceptance, kindness, empathy? How do you feel or what do you think about these changes?

_____

_____

_____

_____

_____

_____

_____

_____

_____

_____

_____

_____

_____

August 24

"Gratitude is the best attitude. There is not a more pleasing exercise of the mind than gratitude. It is accompanied with such an inward satisfaction that the duty is sufficiently rewarded by the performance."

~ Joseph Addison

Take a moment and think about your satisfaction with your life since you have been focusing on and practicing gratitude? What do you see different regarding your satisfaction with where you are now and what you have? What do you see is different in how you view and interact with others?

_____

_____

_____

_____

_____

_____

_____

_____

_____

_____

_____

_____

August 25

"When we become more fully aware that our success is due in large measure to the loyalty, helpfulness, and encouragement we have received from others, our desire grows to pass on similar gifts. Gratitude spurs us on to prove ourselves worthy of what others have done for us. The spirit of gratitude is a powerful energizer."

~ Wilferd A. Peterson

Describe what is different about you energetically and how you now face the day; your work/career/business; your relationships? How are you living life differently and how are others reacting to these changes?

_____

_____

_____

_____

_____

_____

_____

_____

_____

_____

_____

_____

_____

August 26

> *"Gratitude is one of the least articulate of the emotions,*
> *especially when it is deep."*

~ *Felix Frankfurter*

How true….even the concept of gratitude seems more nebulous than some of the other concepts of being and feeling. Perhaps, though the concept has been around for hundreds of years, it is because we are now trying to live it in the present day without it been taught to us as children from the deeper level than just saying "thank you."

Are you finding it difficult to describe the changes, the feelings associated with gratitude? Is this hindering you in a way in moving forward? Are you able to accept what gratitude is doing for you, even if you cannot fully put into words the feelings of gratitude?

_____

_____

_____

_____

_____

_____

_____

_____

_____

_____

_____

_____

_____

August 27

In Memory of My Beloved Late Husband, Alberto Pineda. I am truly grateful that he was in my life, he will FOREVER be in my Heart.

I have walked through fire, survived storms, the rains have seemed endless at times and the earth below my feet has felt unstable, but through this all, I was always taken care of by the universe. As I stood 10,000 feet above sea level on top of Haleakala, feeling the sun come up, I was reminded to have Faith, Patience and Trust because even on the days when one is going through a storm and can't see the sun at sunrise, if we continue to move forward on this path of our Journey in Life, we will come to the point where we do see the sun shine through and life will once again be filled with rainbows. It becomes clear that what seemed like a tragedy at the moment, in reality, is a gift. I've been gifted a second chance in life to now live in receptivity, love, faith and trust. Gratitude is what I wake up with and fall asleep to every day. Lastly, I realize not only has my nightmare ended, but my life has transformed into an amazing life filled with love, joy, purpose, amazing people, days at the beach and just living a dream-filled life on Maui. This is the silver lining that has come from Alberto giving up his life.

Alma Soul Pineda moved to Maui from Los Angeles in 2015. A mother of two amazing young men, she was drawn to Maui, to inspire and help others see the beauty in life through Love, Faith, and Trust. Connect at www.facebook.com/biomatmiraclemaui.

August 28

In Memory of Debra Kay Cude, who taught me to look for silver linings

Living from a place of gratitude, is in essence, living from love, creativity, and passion. The feeling of a grateful heart can be described as paradise found. I find, when I am truly living in gratitude, all I want to do is give it away. The divine connection that is experienced through gratitude is beautiful and awe inspiring. I truly believe, a grateful heart is a giving heart, and that means giving thanks **BEFORE** you receive! From a place of gratitude, there is no want. Gratitude is desire met. Gratitude is your soul dancing. Gratitude will change your life. I encourage you to step into a place of living in gratitude daily.

Lori Ann Foster is a Consultant, Coach, and Mentor with a background in healthcare and professional coaching. She is passionate about personal development, resiliency of the human spirit and living from a place of gratitude. Connect with Lori at contact@lorifostercoaching.com and www.lorifostercoaching.com.

_____

_____

_____

_____

_____

_____

_____

_____

_____

_____

_____

August 29

"A man's indebtedness is not virtue; his repayment is. Virtue begins when he dedicates himself actively, to the job of gratitude."

~ Ruth Benedict

Take a moment and describe your "day of gratitude". Write about your actions, beliefs, interpretations/perspective of people, events and interactions of the day. How often did you realize you were thinking from an "attitude of gratitude" or do you see where you could have been more grateful?

_____

_____

_____

_____

_____

_____

_____

_____

_____

_____

_____

_____

_____

August 30

Happy Day! A friend in Hospice answered her phone this way every day, not just on holidays. You see, she made a **CHOICE** to live each day as a holiday. We can, too. Our emotions are choices. Yes, it is easier to feel positive emotions when we like our circumstances. But if not...yet...deliberately choosing to **FEEL** positive will bring positivity more quickly. How do you do that when things in your life...well, they suck? What feeling do you want to feel? Have you ever felt that way before? Make a list of times in your past when you truly felt grateful. Make that memory into a vivid movie. What did it look like? What did you hear? What were you thinking? Were there any smells associated with it? Smellivision! Did you touch or were you being touched? Can you feel that now? Imagine yourself inside that movie. Be deliberate. Feeling gratitude this way will send out vibrations of gratitude. The Universe can now say, "Oh, I understand what you want. Here's more!" Happy Day! **FEEL** grateful!

Wendy Stout, Ph.D. was a stay at home mom of three who went back to school at age 50 to earn degrees in Natural Healing, including a Ph.D. She leads workshops in EFT (Emotional Freedom Techniques) and the Law of Attraction. Connect with Wendy at https://sway.com/s/OTOBj3K12vZYGy0K/embed.

August 31

"A tree is known by its fruit; a man by his deeds. A good deed is never lost; he who sows courtesy reaps friendship, and he who plants kindness gathers love."

~ Saint Basil

Gratitude results in the growth of not only the person who is living it; it "grows" the people with who it is shared.

What have you noticed about your personal and interpersonal growth since learning about and living in gratitude? What do you notice in the people around you who are also benefitting from your gratitude?

_____

_____

_____

_____

_____

_____

_____

_____

_____

_____

_____

_____

_____

"Be thankful for your body, mind, heart and soul;
Be thankful for your body, it houses and protects
the very essence of who you are;
Be thankful for your mind as it creates your thoughts, emotions,
and decisions;
Be thankful for your heart as it allows you to give and receive love;
and Be thankful for your soul as it is your compass for humanity."

~ Denise Joy Thompson

"Gratitude is the best-kept secret for hundreds of years; unlock this treasure to erase all of your fears."

~ Denise Joy Thompson

September

September 1

"If you concentrate on finding whatever is good in every situation, you will discover that your life will suddenly be filled with gratitude, a feeling that nurtures the soul."

~ Harold Kushner

There is good, or at least not as bad as we think, in every situation. True it may take us a moment to change our perspective from our initial thoughts and reactions to one of acceptance and seeing the "good".

With including gratitude in your life, how has this changed how you perceive, think and act in response to situations which may not seem "good" at the time they are happening? What are you doing now regarding your actions which you were not able to do before?

_____

_____

_____

_____

_____

_____

_____

_____

_____

_____

_____

September 2

"Gratitude is something of which none of us can give too much. For on the smiles, the thanks we give, our little gestures of appreciation, our neighbors build their philosophy of life."

~ A. J. Cronin

With gratitude comes joy, a sense of fun, laughter, smiling, and playfulness. How are you experiencing these? Do you notice a lightness within you? How are people around you responding to you since you have more gratitude? How are you viewing yourself since having more gratitude?

_____

_____

_____

_____

_____

_____

_____

_____

_____

_____

_____

_____

_____

September 3

In Memory of My Late Mother, Mary Ellen Arkward

I never realized the depth of change that would happen after the death of my mother. As a child, I always feared her death, because she was such an important part of my life. She always told me not to fear death; to live life to the fullest after her death. It was a life-changing experience when she died. It was unexpected and sudden. One of the benefits in planning her memorial was we had spoken so often about her wishes. We had shared so much with each other about the existential issues of life and facing death. There were times I thought the pain of missing her was going to completely debilitate me. However, I can honestly say time heals the wounded heart. Confronting death makes you appreciate life. Without death, life would have no meaning. Time allows you to enjoy the memories and to embrace all that was shared. Now more than ever, I realize that I wake up with a greater sense of purpose, a grateful heart because of those that are part of my life. Gratitude allows us to confront the unknown with faith and the knowledge that we lived our best life.

Jean Day has a Master's degree in Clinical Psychology from Pepperdine University, is a college instructor, for 18 years, and a guest expert on numerous radio shows discussing topics about psychology and wellness. Jean is a Nichiren Buddhist and a member of the Soka-Gakkai USA Buddhist organization. Contact Jean at jeanday319@yahoo.com.

September 4

"None of those material possessions do anything to make your life any better... I know a lot of people who have a lot of everything, and they're absolutely the most miserable people in the world. So it won't do anything for you unless you're a happy person and can have peace with yourself."

~ Lenny Kravitz

How true, we see homeless people who are content and happy, and we see millionaires who are miserable. It is like seeing a child with lots of toys, and they are happily creating a fort with a box! We often equate happiness, self-fulfillment with material possessions; we are filling a void with stuff. The HGTV shows of Tiny Houses shows we do not need the mansion to live comfortably.

With your new Live In Gratitude Daily lifestyle, what do you no longer "need" to have? What are you not spending money on? What are you not buying which before seemed necessary? How is this changing your life?

September 5

"Bad things do happen; how I respond to them defines my character and the quality of my life. I can choose to sit in perpetual sadness, immobilized by the gravity of my loss, or I can choose to rise from the pain and treasure the most precious gift I have—life itself."

~ Walter Anderson

Yes, even when we live in gratitude we will still have loss, pain, disappointment. With gratitude though we also can more quickly move forward and not allow people or situations to hold us down or back from living in the joy of gratitude, while also acknowledging the difficulties which occur in life.

Think about how you have responded to difficult situations since incorporating gratitude in your life. What was different about your response? How long did any negative or uncomfortable emotions remain before you were able to change your perspective and to think of the situation? How do you feel about yourself and your progress with gratitude regarding your responses?

_____

_____

_____

_____

_____

_____

_____

_____

_____

_____

_____

September 6

These are the **Symptoms of Inner Peace** I experienced and continue to hold to:

- Thinking and acting deliberately from the point of joy and not fear
- Loss of interest in judging others and myself
- Tendency to allow things to unfold rather than resisting or controlling them
- Increased frequency of unexpected smiling
- The ability to enjoy each moment and challenge
- Overwhelming episodes of appreciation
- Loss of interest in conflict
- Loss of interest in worry
- Feelings of connectedness with others and nature
- Susceptibility to kindness and an uncontrollable urge to reciprocate

So, my offering to you is that when you feel the pressures of life, and you will, take a moment to expand your awareness to the other truths present. Lock into what is good with everything you are and things will shift. And remember; there is just one river of life: You can choose to float on it or fight against it….**FLOAT ON!**

Sharlene Trumet LMT, CWC, CLC, has 22 years of assisting people with their physical, emotional and spiritual well-being. Connect with Sharlene at www.livnbetter4ever.com.

_____

_____

_____

_____

_____

_____

_____

_____

_____

September 7

"It isn't what you have in your pocket that makes you thankful, but what you have in your heart."

~ Author Unknown

Gratitude comes back to being heart-centered instead of possession-centered.

How are you leading or acting with your heart, your compassion, your empathy, your acceptance and understanding? What now is more important in your relationships than before becoming more aware of gratitude? How did you show you cared or someone was important to you?

_____

_____

_____

_____

_____

_____

_____

_____

_____

_____

_____

_____

_____

September 8

"Some people are always grumbling because roses have thorns;
I am thankful that thorns have roses."

~ Alphonse Karr

How has your perspective changed overall since incorporating gratitude into your life? Do you see past the "thorns"? Is the "good" or "better" of a situation more obvious now than before? In what areas of your life are you noticing a difference?

_____

_____

_____

_____

_____

_____

_____

_____

_____

_____

_____

_____

_____

September 9

"Joyful is the person who finds wisdom, the one who gains understanding. For wisdom is more profitable than silver, and her wages are better than gold" **Proverbs 3:13-14. NLT**

Be grateful for all your trials in life, because they are not just to make you strong, but to share what you have learned which will strengthen our future generations. Wisdom is one of the many precious gifts we have been blessed by. Never take her for granted, or suppress the lessons she is speaking to you. Shout her aloud to anyone willing to grow, even in their darkest days.

Show your gratitude each time someone is willing to share their life lessons with you.

Lisa Renee Offutt is a native of Indianapolis, Indiana, has worked in customer service for over 25 years and worn several different hats. Lisa is currently studying Psychology, and she plans to work in the area of Forensic Psychology and Christian Counseling. Connect with Lisa at lrenee8508@gmail.com.

_____

_____

_____

_____

_____

_____

_____

_____

_____

_____

_____

_____

September 10

The last three years have been a roller-coaster ride. The end of my 27-year marriage knocked the wind out of me. I was mad. Mad at him. Mad at God for not fixing him/us. As I began to search for answers and try to find my way out of the darkness and pain the words gratitude and grateful kept coming at me from all kinds of sources. Finally, I decided that if nothing else it would make me feel better, maybe for only a few moments but I would take anything. I started a gratitude journal. At first, I could only find a couple of things to write down but soon as I began to write gratitude poured out of me. I was filling pages, and the pain and darkness diminished. I began to wake up with a renewed faith that all was as it should be and I was going to be just fine. When you find things to be grateful for, God will pour blessings over you.

Vickie Washburn is a Teacher, Healer, Coach, and an avid Student of natural healing modalities, spirituality and the root causes of the struggles we all face for the past 30 years. Connect with Vickie at www.vickiewashburn.com.

September 11

As we go through life, our families and careers we don't think that it could all change in a moment. August 9th, 2002 my husband and I were driving to work when we were broadsided by another vehicle. The vehicle hit us just in front of the passenger door, a little further back and I would not be writing this today. Some may consider this a tragic moment, and at the time I did too. Today I am grateful not only for surviving the accident but that during my recovery my doctors found I had some undiagnosed medical problems that could have been serious if left untreated. I turned 50 on September 11th the following year. I had my daughter throw me a big birthday party, after all, I nearly missed it. We never know what tomorrow will bring, today write what you want to do in the future and make it something you do today.

Janet Wiszowaty is a retired Royal Canadian Mounted Police Dispatcher, Internet Radio Show Host of Worldly Connektions and a Visionary Coach/Mentor who is passionate about helping our First Responders who had a trauma/PTSD and are ready to move forward with their life. Follow Janet at www.familyconnekt.com.

September 12

The day after one of the worst days in the history of the US and possibly the world. The terrorist attack on the US seems a long time ago, and yet, it seems like yesterday. The world is different than it was before, I am not sure if it is better or worse, it is definitely different. We cannot know what we or the world would be like without September 11, 2001. What paths were we on before the attack, could something worse have happened? For most of us, we will not make a difference a 'world" level. We can make a difference with ourselves, our family, our community, our state, our country...if we are involved. If we decide to live in a way which promotes acceptance and unity, not dividedness and differences. We have so many freedoms in our country which if always used with the best intent and keeping "our brothers" in mind, it would be amazing what we would create. 9/11 (2001) changed so many lives; now we can create change which would truly honor the lives lost. I am so grateful to be an American; with the freedom and choices given to me. I choose to be grateful, for I have seen the other side of war and it is not the world I want to live in.

Denise Joy Thompson is a Wife, Mother of three furbabies, a #1 International Best-Selling Author, Coach, Colonel in the Air Force Reserve, a Therapist, and Veteran. She is the host of The Power Of A Woman's Voice TV show. Denise's mission is for everyone to have the life they can create. Connect with Denise at thecoachalliance@gmail.com and www.facebook.com/gp/LiveInGrattiudeDaily.

_____

_____

_____

_____

_____

_____

_____

_____

_____

_____

September 13

"Gratitude doesn't change the scenery. It merely washes clean the glass you look through so you can clearly see the colors."

~ Richelle E. Goodrich

How are you seeing/viewing life differently with gratitude? What is different about the "lens" through which you observe and assess your life, your relationships, the situations you are involved in? How is gratitude changing your perspective? How is gratitude changing your thoughts and feelings about your life?

_____

_____

_____

_____

_____

_____

_____

_____

_____

_____

_____

_____

_____

_____

September 14

"It's the recognition that other people's problems, their pain and frustrations, are every bit as real as our own – often far worse. In recognizing this fact and trying to offer some assistance, we open our hearts and greatly enhance our sense of gratitude."

~ Richard Carlson

Gratitude opens our heart, mind, and spirit to experience and feel raw emotion on a much deeper level. This is part of the transformation which occurs when we **Live In Gratitude Daily**. If everyone were in "gratitude", there would not be wars, abuse or criminal activity. Those behaviors are counterintuitive to gratitude, and they cannot co-exist.

What emotions are you experiencing on a deeper level, how are you responding to those changes? How are you handling this change and do you have someone to share this with? (If not join our FB group **Live in Gratitude Daily** for support)

_____

_____

_____

_____

_____

_____

_____

_____

_____

_____

_____

_____

September 15

In Honor of My Sacred Marriage to My Loving Wife, Janis

Today we wake up to a new dawn within, one that is filled with possibilities that are endless and fueled by a power much greater than this earth. We are not limited by what we can see, hear, feel or even touch. When we are still, we tap into the world where there are love and light that fills our hearts and beckons us to listen. In this love, we have the power to be the future that we dream for the next generation and beyond. Let go and surrender into the possibility that all is exactly the way it is supposed to be in the moment. Tap into the authentic self which is peace and love and let go of your old stories of what could have, would have, and should have. Today I take full responsibility for my new life, because I woke up, healthy and able to breathe, in this beautiful nation. I am grateful for where I am and where I can choose to go next.

Laura Goodman The Shameless Warrior(tm) is the embodiment of reverent authentic love. Her mission is to lend her voice to Warriors of abuse who have not found theirs. Laura is an Author, Mentor, Warrior, Teacher, Speaker, and Advocate. She is here to serve humanity and loves with an open heart, fully and completely. Connect with Laura at www.facebook.com/pg/shamelesswarrior.

September 16

"A good life is when you smile often, dream big, laugh a lot and realize how blessed you really are."

~ Unknown

My transformational journey started several years ago. One of the choices I made was to attend a Laughter Yoga Leader course. Yes, I learned to laugh, more accurately I learned how to lead others in laughter. I was blessed to experience this focused time on laughter and joy. The additional blessing was the like-minded, heart-centered people I met.

Think about your gratitude journey. Are you experiencing more laughter, are you smiling more, is this noticed by other people? If so what is their reaction? Are they smiling and laughing more too? How does this make you feel?

_____

_____

_____

_____

_____

_____

_____

_____

_____

_____

_____

_____

September 17

"Gratitude is absolutely the way to bring more into your life."

~ Unknown

What has gratitude brought into your life? More joy, personal interaction, contentment? Another way to look at this is what is there less of? Is there less discontent? Is there less anxiety and sadness? Is there less loneliness? Gratitude can bring so much positivity to your life, the less wanted emotions and situations can fade away, sometimes we don't even notice they were ever there.

_____

_____

_____

_____

_____

_____

_____

_____

_____

_____

_____

_____

_____

_____

_____

_____

September 18

"Well, Angela, your labs look good, very good – you're **CURED!**"

Regardless of the alarming statistics, no one should ever have to hear the words "you have cancer." And I heard those words at age 13 in 1984. But after a summer of radiation treatments, hair loss, major surgery, and feeling all too familiar with needles and other known tests only a hospital can provide, on September 18th, 1989 I was proclaimed CURED. I received a different outlook on life, unfortunately, while still being too young and immature to appreciate it! Fast forward to today– I get it. Although I was in my early 30s when I experienced many 'a-ha' moments, the day September 18th remains my reminder that life is both about surviving AND thriving. And, for me, the only thing constant…is HOPE.

Jeremiah 29:11 (NIV)
11 For I know the plans I have for you," declares the LORD, "plans to prosper you and not to harm you, plans to give you hope and a future."

Angela Lee graduated from James Madison University ('94), has 20 years working in the IT industry, currently works in the insurance industry and is a Rodan and Fields skincare consultant. Angela is a cancer survivor who advocates for others as a Cancer Action Network ambassador volunteer. Follow Angela at www.facebook.com/angelaglee03.

_____

_____

_____

_____

_____

_____

_____

_____

_____

_____

September 19

Sing the song of Psalms 107:1 "Oh give thanks to the Lord, for he is good, for his steadfast love endures forever." Yes, life will come, and yes the weapons will form, but nothing shall prosper. For when God is in it, there are no limits. Lupus is the title given by the doctors, but God says by his stripes I am healed. You must faith it to make it. You may never know the next person story but know that we all have a story. It's not was written but it about how you live to write it. I am a work in progress, a project under construction and God is not through with me yet. Grateful, "yes I am." I could go on and on and on about your works. Because I'm grateful, grateful, so grateful; just to praise you, Lord. Flowing from my heart are the issues of my heart. It's gratefulness." Never give up, never give into fear; for God has not given us the spirit of fear. Know that we all have been given an assignment of purpose, we must walk by faith and not by sight. I am a living testimony, a child of the most high, victorious. I am of a royal lineage, and I must walk in my Queen-ship. I have eyes watching, and they are my reason for wanting what God has for me.

Jada Andrews is a God-fearing Mother, Daughter, Disabled Veteran & Business Owner, who's taken the challenges of life and turned them into stepping stones towards greatness. She is the owner of A Mustard Seed, she puts God first and walks in victory. Connect with Jada at www.facebook.com/AMustardSeed75

September 20

Overcoming a challenging childhood to become the parent I wanted to be required faith in the seemingly impossible, determination to push past my programming, and surrendering to a complete mindset overhaul. The most profound component of my new mindset was Gratitude.

Five years later, with two little boys and a parent mentoring business, Sami's Voice, I teach gratitude daily. One gratitude practice I teach is to flip frustrating behaviors into positive attributes parents can be grateful their children have. A bossy child becomes "a confident leader". A destructive child becomes "creative and science oriented". An overly sensitive (whiny) child becomes "empathetic and intuitive." Once the characteristics are newly framed, the parent's job simplifies. Rather than the job of ending children's innate tendencies, parents are instead tasked with honing the skills that will make them uniquely successful. They teach their children how to appropriately use their gifts. After all, guiding is far less daunting than changing.

The gratitude found in this shift leads to understanding, understanding garners respect, respect proceeds appreciation, and appreciation highlights further reasons for gratitude. This beautiful cycle encases the family in love.

Samantha Bell is a Mother, Licensed Teacher, Parenting Mentor, and the Creator of Sami's Voice. Her mission is empowering mothers to parent calmly, confidently, and connectedly to create a better childhood for every child. www.samisvoice.com.

_____

_____

_____

_____

_____

_____

_____

_____

_____

_____

September 21

Years ago while driving in a city, an octagon shaped high-rise building attracted my attention. "Someday we'll live there!" I told my husband. A month later we moved and took jobs as Residential Managers which included a place to live, on the 18th floor of that octagon shaped high-rise building! From then on, I used that technique frequently to achieve goals both large and small. Over 20 years later I learned about RAS.

The Reticular Activating System (RAS), is how our brain takes in, filters and compartmentalizes information and decides what to reject, mark for immediate/near future use or hold for future recall.

Activating the RAS for gratitude is as simple as writing down, reading and revising long-term and short-term goals each morning. The RAS will match any information important to achieving your goals. Soon you'll begin noticing important ways to fulfill your goals because you're more aware. Your gratitude will also grow because you are achieving things you desire in your life.

Try it. It works!

Judith Richardson Schroeder, a Sub-conscious Behaviorist and Life Enhancement Coach, helps clients uncover their inner gifts and teaches them how to foster a life of true gratitude and fulfillment. Her favorite pastime though is spending time with her beautiful granddaughter, Arya. Connect with Judith at www.guidancefromwithincoaching.com

September 22

"Appreciation can make a day, even change a life. Your willingness to put it into words is all that is necessary."

~ Unknown

We know words saves lives; communication is a foundational element of all relationships. Expressing appreciation, and thankfulness is one of the foundational elements of living a life of gratitude.

How are you expressing appreciation, not only in words but also in actions? What are you comfortable with saying or doing and what would be a stretch for you to say or do? Whatever is a stretch, work on adding it to your Live In Gratitude Daily lifestyle.

_____

_____

_____

_____

_____

_____

_____

_____

_____

_____

_____

_____

September 23

"Each day I am grateful for nights turned into mornings,
Friends that turned into family,
Dreams that turned into reality and
Likes that turned into love."

~ Unknown

What are you grateful for what happened or you experienced today?   What are you grateful for regarding you, personally?

_____

_____

_____

_____

_____

_____

_____

_____

_____

_____

_____

_____

_____

_____

September 24

"No duty is more urgent than that of returning thanks."

~ James Allen

Life is hectic, and we often get caught up with the demands of busy schedules. If you miss an opportunity to say thank you, how do make up for it?

What steps do you take to remember to give thank you? How do you make sure you are expressing appreciation and gratitude? Is there anything you have had difficulty giving thanks for?

_____

_____

_____

_____

_____

_____

_____

_____

_____

_____

_____

_____

_____

Sept 25

In Dedication to a man I have known and loved all of my adult life, My Husband Arthur Taylor, the Father of My Son

Years ago when he was chasing me in high school, I would not have thought he would have been the person who would influence my life as a woman first, wife, mother and a professional. I am thankful to God and him that we have spent all of our adult life together as friends, partners, and parents.

I live in gratitude because of all the young lives he and I had impacted, being there for many when their parent was not, assisting with their education and employment opportunities too. I live in gratitude how he has taught our son the importance of helping others. I am truly grateful for the respect and belief he has in the equality of women and their abilities to do and be whatever she chooses. I am also so grateful to God for whatever reason his severe illness did not result in death.

Geraldine Taylor is a Health and Wellness Director at a senior living facility and is the Deputy Executive Director for ImpactSM Charity Inc.; a family owned 501(c3). She is also an Organo Gold Independent Distributor. Contact Geraldine at nitro2221@gmail.com

September 26

"Life is an echo. What you send out, comes back. What you sow, you reap. What you give, you get. What you see in others, exists in you. Remember, life is an echo. It always gets back to you. So give goodness. "

~ Unknown

It can be hard at times to see the goodness and be the goodness because we are human. We are able to "course correct" and get back on track as soon as possible, though. Once you recognize what echo you are receiving and sending, decide if you need to switch to more goodness.

Since we cannot be in gratitude 100% how do you "course correct" when you are not in gratitude? What brings you back to gratitude?

_____

_____

_____

_____

_____

_____

_____

_____

_____

_____

_____

September 27

"Kindness in words creates confidence. Kindness in thinking creates profoundness. Kindness in giving creates love."

~ Lao Tzu

There is so much goodness in each one us, though we are not all on a similar journey at the same time. Our one responsibility is to be the best person we can be, regardless of what someone else is doing. We, who are on the **Live In Gratitude Daily** journey, are more capable of taking the "high road" to kindness than others might be. It is ok, if we do not at the moment receive kindness, it will come in time with our continued living in gratitude. Our knowing we are grateful and kind is reward enough.

How do stay in gratitude when faced with a lack of kindness or appreciation from others? What is about your experience with gratitude which is comforting and motivates you to be grateful for any experience you encounter?

_____

_____

_____

_____

_____

_____

_____

_____

_____

_____

_____

September 28

"We live in deeds, not years; in thoughts, not figures on a dial. We should count time by heart-throbs. He most lives who thinks most, feels the noblest, acts the best."

~ Phillip James Bailey

What are your gratitude deeds? How are you sharing your gratitude with others?

_____

_____

_____

_____

_____

_____

_____

_____

_____

_____

_____

_____

_____

_____

_____

_____

September 29

"How easily we can forget how precious life is! So long as we can remember, we've just been here, being alive. Unlike other things for which we have a good comparison– black to white, day to night, good to bad– we are so immersed in life that we can see it only in the context of itself. We don't see life as compared to anything, to not-being, for example, to never having been born. Life just is. But life itself is a gift. It's a compliment just being born: to feel, breathe, think, play, dance, sing, work, make love, for this particular lifetime. Today, let's give thanks for life. For life itself. For simply being born!"

~ Daphne Rose Kingma

Gratitude is not only about how we are grateful and thank others; it is about celebrating, loving and thanking ourselves too!!
How are you giving thanks for the very fact you are alive? How are you celebrating you?

_____

_____

_____

_____

_____

_____

_____

_____

_____

_____

_____

September 30

Share a moment (or people) in your life (or business) for which you are grateful.

The moments for which I am most grateful are when individuals pleasantly surprise me by surpassing my expectations of what I hoped would transpire in a business or personal relationship; it is during moments like these that my faith in the human race is bolstered. In these trying times of political and economic uncertainty and global strife, I am deeply grateful to be fortunate enough to be surrounded by such wonderful people who I am thrilled to call my friends and associates.

Jeanette B. Marco is Executive Director at MarcoArt New York, is a Get Reel TV Show Host, is Editor in Chief of En' Route Middle East and Cachet Travels USA. Connect with Jeanette at www.itsabeautifullife.us.

"Gratitude is the key to all your heart and soul desires; daily appreciation and "thank yous" are all that life requires."

~ Denise Joy Thompson

October

October 1

In Dedication to Esther Miguel, without you, I wouldn't be here today

I'm grateful for the opportunity to live on Maui, Hawaii. This opportunity has given me a second chance at life and introduced me to life changing people. People who have helped lead me back to me, which is LOVE. LOVE and GRATITUDE go hand in hand. My Maui Ohana I will forever be grateful to, and they will always be in my heart.

I'm grateful that here not only have I learned to love myself, but I've learned to dance, sing, enjoy life once more. I've learned to truly SEE life for what it is. It's being PRESENT at every moment and being GRATEFUL for those moments.

I'm grateful to myself for saying "YES" to living life to the fullest and seeing Heaven on Earth in my daily life!

Alma Soul Pineda moved to Maui, Hi from Los Angeles, CA in 2015. She embodies the Aloha spirit. A mother of two amazing young men, she was drawn to Maui, to inspire and help others see the beauty in life through Love, Faith, and Trust. She also envisions the world being able to heal holistically. Contact Alma at https://thebiomatmiracle.com.

October 2

In Dedication to My Mom, Bonnie Joy Thompson (DOB Oct 1)

My mom is truly loved by our whole family. She not only "mothered" my brother and me, she also spent numerous days watching her two oldest granddaughters and now at 80, has the twin granddaughters at her house 1-2 days a week, which benefits all three of them with the relationship they are building. My mom, with my dad as the traditional husband, father, and bread-winner, is the glue which held everything together. She was always available with help and support as needed; she made our house a home, she provided the mothering and spoiling which is gratefully appreciated. I was never told I could not accomplish anything; I was never held back from learning, exploring or making my way in the world. I was never degraded or talked down to; my skills, talents, and intellect were never questioned or doubted. My mom was able to work with me and who I was as a child, adolescent, adult instead of demanding I be someone I was not. There were no limits placed on my capabilities, only encouragement and support of my endeavors.

Denise Joy Thompson is a Wife, Mother of three furbabies, a #1 International Best-Seller Author, Coach, Colonel in the Air Force Reserve, a Therapist, and Veteran. She is the host of The Power Of A Woman's Voice TV show. Denise's mission is for everyone to have the life they can create. Connect with Denise at thecoachalliance@gmail.com and www.facebook.com/gp/LiveInGrattiudeDaily.

October 3

Dedicated to My Husband who regularly reminds me how blessed I am

The other night I walked into my bedroom after work and saw a big stack of clothes I needed to put away. I was tired and started complaining in my head. "I don't want to do this", "I just want to get into comfy clothes and sit down", "How long is this going to take?" You get the picture.

Then I did something that completely changed the way I felt! I flipped the script! Instead of complaining, I started thinking of all the things I was thankful for related to the clothes. Thankful I had clothes to choose from, Thankful that we have water and soap so I can wear clean clothes, Thankful that I am physically able to put them away, and continued until what seemed like hardly any time at all in all the clothes were put away.

I am so happy and grateful to for my clothes because _____ .

Allison "FAB" Howell- social worker by day, Life Stylist by night teaching women to feel FABulous in Life & Style. Allison combines experience in fashion and psychology to inspire lives to be fun, fresh, and full of FABulous love. www.FABover.com.

_____

_____

_____

_____

_____

_____

_____

_____

_____

_____

_____

_____

October 4

"When you rise in the morning, give thanks for the light, for your life, for your strength. Give thanks for your food and for the joy of living. If you see no reason to give thanks, the fault lies in yourself."

~ Tecumseh

As you rise this morning or as you ready for sleep tonight, what are you giving thanks for today?

_____

_____

_____

_____

_____

_____

_____

_____

_____

_____

_____

_____

_____

_____

_____

_____

October 5

"The one thing all humans have in common is that each of us wants to be happy; and happiness is born from gratitude."

~ Brother David Steindl-Rast

How are you experiencing happiness each day? How are you seeing your gratitude increasing your happiness?

_____

_____

_____

_____

_____

_____

_____

_____

_____

_____

_____

_____

_____

_____

October 6

*"Take time to be thankful for everything you have,
you could have more and you could have a lot less."*

~ Unknown

What are the top ten things you are thankful for today?

(After you write down the top ten, write down ten more!!)

_____

_____

_____

_____

_____

_____

_____

_____

_____

_____

_____

_____

_____

_____

_____

October 7

> *"When you think things are bad,*
> *when you feel sour and blue,*
> *when you start to get mad...*
> *you should do what I do!*
> *Just tell yourself, Duckie,*
> *you're really quite lucky!*
> *Some people are much more...*
> *oh, ever so much more...*
> *oh, muchly much-much more*
> *unlucky than you!"*
>
> *~Dr. Seuss*

Even Dr. Seuss is on the gratitude game!! We can be grateful for what we have, there is so much abundance in the world, and we do have quite a bit of it.

When you are feeling low, or as if the weight of the world is on your shoulders, what gratitude thoughts brings you back to a feeling of contentment, satisfaction, and appreciation?

_____

_____

_____

_____

_____

_____

_____

_____

_____

_____

October 8

Dedicated to My Kitty, Izzy

I am grateful I learned the art of loving another being. Interestingly, I learned it from my cat. The love I feel has no expectations or conditions attached. It is a profoundly deep gratitude I receive after I have been loving to another, and especially to Izzy. She's my 10-year old feral kitty who would not let me touch her even two months after I got her. Craving affection, I got another cat; Emily. Izzy became more defiant and distant until Emily ran away one night. The change was remarkable! Izzy became affectionate, allowing me to pet her. Now, we have our special petting routine, and my heart swells with love and gratitude when she allows me to run my hand from her head and ears to the tip of her tail. I am ecstatic she allows me to touch her this way.

The lesson of gratitude can be gained from any being, as Izzy has demonstrated. Become aware of others from which to learn this practice and you can transform your life.

Carolyn CJ Jones is an Award-winning Author, Speaker, Forgiveness Coach, and a Retired Registered Nurse. At fifty-eight, she overcame the anger and bitterness she'd lived with her entire adult life when she discovered forgiveness and gratitude. As a result, she experiences great peace and freedom in her life. Contact CJ at carolyncjjones.com

October 9

Dedicated to My Special Girlfriends, especially Kim Witherspoon, and to My Mentors, especially Daisaku Ikeda

In discussing gratitude, one of the most significant moments of my life was becoming a Nichiren Buddhist. Buddhism changed not only my life and my heart; it has enriched my life in ways that I could not have imagined. There are countless friends, in my Buddhist community, who have supported and nourished my soul. As a single woman, my friends are like family to me. I turn to them for support, advice, and love. My best friend, Kim Witherspoon, has heard my deepest secrets, my fears, my dreams and all the complexities that reflect me. I can say, without a doubt, my girlfriends are the treasures of my heart. I carry their hearts; I carry them in my heart. My purpose is to be that mentor to others, to be that friend, that person that is the beacon of light to others. To carry the burdens of others is my higher purpose. Because of my practice of Buddhism and with the help of my girlfriends, I have greater compassion, a greater sense of mission, and freedom to be a better woman.

Jean Day has a Master's degree in Clinical Psychology from Pepperdine University, is a College Instructor, of 18 years, and a Guest Expert on numerous radio shows discussing topics about psychology and wellness. Jean is a Nichiren Buddhist and a member of the Soka-Gakkai USA Buddhist organization. Contact Jean at jeanday319@yahoo.com.

October 10

When it comes to love, I am a **hopeless romantic**. Despite two messy divorces, I always believed in finding the perfect mate and living happily ever after. So, when the woman who is my **soulmate** magically appeared in my mid-40's, I knew that I was finally ready for true love.

The only glitch was the fact that we could not get married. To me, marriage is a wonderful ritual and symbol to the world of a couple's commitments to nurturing their love. It seemed cruelly ironic that I could not have that with the one person I believed I was destined to spend the rest of my life with.

I am so grateful to all of the gay rights activists and organizations who fought and advocated and struggled to **legalize gay marriage**. As soon as our home state of Massachusetts made it possible for us to marry legally, we set a date for October 10, 2008. Every day I thank the Universe for honoring and blessing our love.

Laurie Morin is a Law Professor, Activist, Entrepreneur, and Change-maker. She leads retreats where people reconnect with their passions and forgotten dreams, and design a plan to create more joy, meaning, and satisfaction in their lives. Connect with Laurie at www.lauriemorin.com.

October 11

"Gratitude doesn't have to be a serious matter! If you want to thank someone, do it by putting a smile on their face or even making them laugh."

~ Unknown

How often are you smiling and laughing know you are living a gratitude-filled life? How do smiling and laughing make you feel? If you haven't laughed or smiled in a while, do it now, yes, right now. If you can make yourself smile and laugh you will do great at helping others to do so.

_____

_____

_____

_____

_____

_____

_____

_____

_____

_____

_____

_____

_____

_____

_____

October 12

"Though I am grateful for the blessings of wealth, it hasn't changed who I am. My feet are still on the ground. I'm just wearing better shoes."

~ Oprah Winfrey

Gratitude doesn't change our inner being; it allows the truly loving being to come out? **How has gratitude changed your outlook for the better while you are still being you?**

_____

_____

_____

_____

_____

_____

_____

_____

_____

_____

_____

_____

_____

_____

_____

_____

October 13

"You ought to be thankful a hole heaping lot, for
The places and people you're lucky you're not!"

~ Dr. Seuss

More thankfulness and gratitude creates happiness and joy. There are people who are not aware of the benefits and blessings of gratitude, for you on this journey you will be blessed beyond measure from what you receive from living in gratitude. Your light of gratitude can shine for others who are not so fortunate to be where you are and where you are going.

What are the blessings and benefits you have already received since increasing gratitude in your life?

_____

_____

_____

_____

_____

_____

_____

_____

_____

_____

_____

_____

_____

October 14

Dedication To the Heroes and Sheroes of My Life

I am often grateful for the many people in my life, who have helped formed me, supported me through my life journey. I am the person I am today because many people have been present for me especially during times of my milestones of life lessons. For me, Gratitude is a state of being that I choose each day to develop as a part of my unique being. This year on October 15, I decided to sing *"The Wind Beneath My Wings,"* my favorite song, especially when I think of the first Heroes/Sheroes in my life, my beloved parents, in my church Fall Fest. In April of 2016, the Sharing of a parent with Special Needs Child, 50 years fight with "normal "society system to provide equal opportunities that his child could have just keep nudging me. I know that fight well. Beyond the US, I have fought that for at least 20 years in the Asia region. It was indeed a privilege I could sing through before I broke down in tears. What is your passion?

Martha Chua is a transplant to Mississippi from Singapore. Life journey towards light is her life pursuit of purpose, wisdom, and enlightenment to inspire others with her unique life lessons learned and experienced and to be a difference in lives of others. Connect with Martha at lifejourneytowardslight@gmail.com.

October 15

"I want to say thank you to all the people who walked into my life and made it outstanding, and all the people who walked out of my life and made it fantastic."

~ Unknown

Who are you grateful for in your life right now? What are the lessons you have learned from those who have left and how are you grateful for those lessons?

_____

_____

_____

_____

_____

_____

_____

_____

_____

_____

_____

_____

_____

_____

October 16

"I am thankful for laughter, except when milk comes out of my nose."

~ Woody Allen

Laughter is the best medicine!!

Laughter was mentioned earlier, if you missed it, it will come around again. How does laughter make you feel? What are you grateful for that makes you laugh?

_____

_____

_____

_____

_____

_____

_____

_____

_____

_____

_____

_____

_____

_____

_____

_____

October 17

In Gratitude for My Daughter, Courtney

For as long as I can remember my one constant dream was that I would someday be a mommy. So much that unlike many of my friends, I continued to play with my baby dolls into my early teens. In 1984, at the age of 30, I met the love of my life who shared my dream to parent and we married shortly after.

After about four years and two ectopic pregnancies, it began to look as though becoming a mommy through my own pregnancy was not going to happen. We found an adoption agency and began the process. Eighteen months later, our beautiful baby girl was born on October 17, 1990. From the first moment I saw her, it was love. And when I held her in my arms, I knew my life was blessed in a way even more beautiful than my life long dreams could have ever conceived. Every day I thank God for my baby girl who continues to make my dreams come true.

Colleen Shade is the owner of *E3 Virtual Assist. Connect with Colleen at* www.facebook.com/E3VirtualAssist, COShade.SOC@gmail.com, www.linkedin.com/in/e3virtualassistcoshade *and* E3VirtualAssist@gmail.com

October 18

"You have no cause for anything but gratitude and joy."

~ Buddha

We can choose our lifestyle and mindset, why would we no want to focus on gratitude and joy? The world around us seems to focus on lack, discontent, and dissatisfaction. We are created to love; we are created to be grateful to see the good to enjoy life. We can live that lifestyle if we choose to do.

What choices are you making? What changes have you made in your life since starting the Live In Gratitude Daily lifestyle? What are additional ways you can add even more gratitude and joy in your life?

_____

_____

_____

_____

_____

_____

_____

_____

_____

_____

_____

_____

October 19

In Dedication to My Dad and Mom

I really do have the best parents! (it is ok, others say this also). My parents chose to adopt and in doing so provided me with one of the best homes possible. Our life was not perfect, we were not rich, and at times money was tight. There was love, encouragement, support and always a listening ear. These parents were chosen for me, God knew who needed me, and He knew they were the right dad and mom to raise me. I am blessed to have had a wonderful childhood and today, even with my dad being in Heaven, I know I am loved beyond measure and I always will be. This is the most important blessing I am given from my parents.

Denise Joy Thompson is a Wife, Mother of three furbabies, a #1 International Best-Seller Author, Coach, Colonel in the Air Force Reserve, a Therapist, and Veteran. She is the host of The Power Of A Woman's Voice TV show. Denise's mission is for everyone to have the life they want. Connect with Denise at thecoachalliance@gmail.com and www.facebook.com/gp/LiveInGrattiudeDaily.

October 20

In Dedication of My Birthday

The day we are born we come with many gifts that we can utilize and share with others. One gift I am grateful for is to have been bestowed a FORGIVING heart. This gift has been my life saver. My story has not been the worst but not the prettiest either. I have had to forgive so many people along the way, including myself, in order live a prosperous life. I cannot imagine where I would be if I held on to the ANGER and the BITTERNESS of the past. We hold the power to forgive others. The sooner we choose to let go of anger, grudges and hurt the sooner we can start the healing process. I know for some people it may hard to forgive quickly, and that is okay. Only the person who has been hurt knows the depth of hurt the offender has caused. I challenge you today to forgive and live the happy life you were born to live! Be in gratitude for your life.

Angelica Solis is an Entrepreneur and Realtor in Texas. Angie loves to travel, experience life at its fullest and is always open to new adventures. Connect with Angelica Solis at www.facebook.com/Angierealtor2016.

October 21

"It's amazing how two words can mean so much...Thank you."

~ Unknown

How many times do you remember saying thank you today? To whom did you say it? Thinking back over the day were there more times it could have been said? For tomorrow see if you say it even more because you are more aware of thinking about it today.

October 22

"Happiness cannot be traveled to, owned, earned or worn. It is the spiritual experience of living every minute with love, grace, and gratitude."

~ Denis Waitley

What are you happy about today? How is this connected or related to the gratitude you are creating in your life?

_____

_____

_____

_____

_____

_____

_____

_____

_____

_____

_____

_____

_____

_____

_____

_____

October 23

I am most grateful for relationships: my relationship with God (wisdom), self and others.

Some of the most profound lessons toward Freedom have been learning to:
1. Focus on Self, center in spirit.
2. What is my perspective?
3. What is their perspective?
4. How can we both win?
5. Take time to think and process.
6. What would honor _____?
7. Whose is it?

Magic happens when: 1. We admit out loud to another human being, our stuff; 2. Seek wisdom; 3. Check for confirmation in 3 places; 4. Does your "Skin" fit? (not necessarily comfortable)

I appreciate giving full makeovers inside and out! Makeovers are meaning, reflecting YOU!

Sheila Hildebrand is a Wife and Mother to 3 adult children. She has been a Cosmetologist for 35 years and a Business Owner for 30 years. Sheila is a Certified Life/Business Coach and Co-founder of Midwest Military Outreach. She provides workshops and services to Female Veterans to help return to civilian life and the workplace. Follow Sheila at facebook.com/MakeoversinspireAbundanceLlc..

_____

_____

_____

_____

_____

_____

_____

_____

October 24

"One looks back with appreciation to the brilliant teachers, but with gratitude to those who touched our human feelings. The curriculum is so much necessary raw material, but warmth is the vital element for the growing plant and for the soul of the child."

~ Carl Jung

Who are you grateful for who has touched your heart, who has left a deep emotional message within your soul? What is the lesson of gratitude you learned from them?

_____

_____

_____

_____

_____

_____

_____

_____

_____

_____

_____

_____

_____

_____

_____

October 25

In Honor of a Beautiful Day

In 2006, I had just learned to walk again, following a slip and fall in my home. Being independent was all that was on my mind as I went through the arduous physical therapy. Once I could drive again, I was elated!

Getting out of the van after my first adventure to the store, I experienced pain in my knee so desperate; it took my breath away. My aide told me to relax that she'd help me in a minute. All I could do was stand there, looking at the sunshine pouring through the trees, surrounded by bright blue skies. I felt honored to be outside with all that beauty.

The more I appreciated where I was, the lighter I felt. Without even realizing it, I began to walk, pain-free!

My aide met me at the door with a surprised look on her face. Stammering, she inquired as to how I got into the house without her help. Smiling, I simply reminded her what a beautiful day it was.

*Michigan Native, **Annette Rochelle Aben** is a published Author for over four decades, an Entrepreneur and a Business Owner. Being able to share her enthusiasm for life through her writing is one of her greatest joys. Connect with Annette at www.annetterochelleaben.wordpress.com*

October 26

"Saying thank you is more than good manners.
It is good spirituality."

~ Alfred Agache

How do you feel after saying I thank you? How do you describe the emotion and where is it felt?

How does this feeling encourage to want to say thank you even more?

October 27

Dedicated to My Son, Devon

Firstborn children offer a reciprocal gift of creation, in that a woman becomes a mother with the birth of the child.

Mother wouldn't exist without the child, and child wouldn't exist without the mother. The bond of transition from life to life is sacred.

With that gift comes the awareness of life's fragility. This small being, filled with all the potential of the Universe, is in our hands to be loved, nurtured, protected, guided – yet at every step, we are susceptible to the immense possibility of loss, failure, rejection, and sorrow. There is no relationship that exists like that of mother and child.

I am grateful for this gift of being a Mother. Each day I practice loving and letting go, recognizing in gratitude that both energies can bring me untold ecstatic joy and heartbreaking sadness. So I fearlessly revel in the duality of this joy – its strength and fragility – knowing that love and gratitude are the only true emotions needed to raise our children.

Gayle O Leary is a Gypsy Priestess, trusting the universe on her journey. She is on a quest to gather her tribe as she guides them to remember their Radiant Sacred Selves. Connect with Gayle at Gayle@GayleOLeary.com or Fb.me/RadiantPhoenixInternational

October 28

"Count your blessings, not your woes."

~ Denise Joy Thompson

Have you ever found yourself with friends or co-workers and complaining about everything? Once in a while we need to "vent" 5 seconds is good and then we need to change the course of our thinking, so the "woes" do not continue to grow!!

To see how quickly you can change your thoughts and blessings can out-number woes. Write down one woe, and then ten blessings/gratitudes!! See how quickly this helps us change direction!!

_____

_____

_____

_____

_____

_____

_____

_____

_____

_____

_____

_____

_____

October 29

This date is precious to me for two reasons. It's my father's birthday and it's my first day of active duty in the Air Force. Often as we go through life, we are not aware of the significance of events in our lives. It is commonly in reflection that we see the importance of these events.

I am grateful for my fathers' wisdom. I was overweight as a child. Kids were very cruel, and I was teased daily. My father understood what I was going through and one night he spent a great amount of time consoling me. The one saying he would repeatedly say is, "Kill 'em with kindness." I've kept this piece of advice as it meant no matter how mean people were to me, responding with kindness is always the best option. It has kept me true to who I am. This is not an easy concept to understand as a child or even as an adult. However, it has kept me humble and kind throughout my entire life.

Kimberly Meyers served 26 years in the Air Force; upon retiring she created her fitness business, Fitness Kinektions. She has 24 years' experience as a group fitness instructor, is a certified Leadership Coach, personal trainer and holds an Associates in Kinesiology. Connect with Kimberly at www.fitnesskinektions.com.

October 30

Always present in the heart, Honoring Rita on This Day of Her Birth

I have returned to my home in The Rocky Mountains complete with my souvenir (Hula Girl) from Maui. Before I come back to visit I will have this Hula down so I can dance like there is nobody watching! My heart was deepened by this experience in a way that can only be expressed in love. I was able to speak with confidence as a leader of my global message that I was born on this earth to deliver. I have the confidence now to move forward and move people and create these safe places for women to find their voices. 2016 was my year, and it is profound the shifts that have found their way to my heart due to my beautiful experiences on the sacred island of Maui with Marsh Engle and the One Million Called to Lead initiative. I am grateful to "my sisters of Maui" for their acceptance, encouragement, and love.

Laura Goodman The Shameless Warrior(tm) is the embodiment of reverent authentic love. Her mission is to lend her voice to Warriors of abuse who have not found theirs. Laura is an Author, Mentor, Warrior, Teacher, Speaker, Advocate. She is here to serve humanity and loves with an open heart, fully and completely. Connect with Laura at /www.facebook.com/pg/shamelesswarrior.

October 31

*"To educate yourself for the feeling of gratitude means
to take nothing for granted."*

~ *Albert Schweitzer*

This is what you are doing, educating yourself on gratitude, by living it and examining it every day.

What are the lessons on gratitude you have learned? What are you no longer taking for granted?

_____

_____

_____

_____

_____

_____

_____

_____

_____

_____

_____

_____

_____

_____

"Gratitude is one of the simplest acts;
The value of which is priceless."

~ Denise Joy Thompson

"Gratitude is not only for the moment in time;
Gratitude is for a lifetime."

~ Denise Joy Thompson

November

November 1

We are ¾'s through 2017. It's difficult to move forward if we are looking behind. What hasn't panned out this year? What are your disappointments & regrets? Regrets are like magnets for more mistakes and missteps. Own what hasn't worked and FORGIVE YOURSELF - Course Correct & Move Forward!!

Then your Daily Gratitude will support your Intentions & Endeavors. A clearer road will be laid for your Manifestations & Abundance. Then and Only then can God/The Universe conspire to work with you to create your Best Life! FORGIVE, COURSE CORRECT, BE GRATEFUL, BE ABUNDANT!!

Brenda B. Bailey is a Certified Belief Integration Specialist, Coach, and Consultant. Connect with Brenda at www.facebook.com/unlimitedpossibilities101.com and www.UnlimitedPossibilities101.com.

November 2

In Dedication of My Siblings

Today I am grateful for my siblings. They have been there to help guide, lead, and support me in everyday life and into my adulthood. They are each incredible role models and make a difference in our family, their families, friends, and relatives. They are true leaders and brighten up the lives of others just by being the special individuals that they are. 1 John 4:21 And He (the Lord) has given us this command: Whoever loves God must also love his brother. (NIV) Ephesians 4:32 Be kind and compassionate to one another, forgiving each other, just as Christ forgave you. (NIV)

What childhood and/or adulthood memories are you grateful for?

DeLyla Haunschild is a Mother to two and a College Graduate. DeLyla's faith is the one constant that remains throughout her life; she knows she has so many blessings to be grateful and thankful to the Lord for experiencing. Follow DeLyla at www.facebook.com/DeLylaHaunschild or email at DeLyla.Global.247@gmail.com.

November 3

"Feeling grateful or appreciative of someone or something
in your life actually attracts more of the things that you appreciate
and value into your life."

~ Christiane Northrup

With living in gratitude, what do you see in your life now that you did not have or possibly did not notice? Your energy and vibration of gratitude are bringing more into your life? Take a moment and see what has been given and received?

_____

_____

_____

_____

_____

_____

_____

_____

_____

_____

_____

_____

_____

November 4

In Dedication to My Husband

This was the last day of my life that I would have to walk this earth alone. Brandon, I have never been more positive that you and I were divinely planned to do life together. I'm grateful for our crazy story and how we ended up here. Daily, I am grateful that you walk out the door to work hard for your family, putting your life on the line to do what you love and serve your community. I'm grateful for the sacrifices that you make for us and how much you love our son. No matter what life throws at us, I'm so glad that we will get to trudge through it together. Most of all, I'm grateful that you love me unconditionally. Thank you for always supporting me and my crazy ideas. You've made me a better person and I'm forever grateful for you being mine. I L.O.V.E. You.

Brittany L. Sumner is a Wife to a wonderful husband, Mother to a rambunctious son and Business Owner at www.crazywinelady.com. She has a passion for helping others, serving her church and enjoying a good glass of wine.

November 5

*"The spiritual journey is the unlearning of fear
and the acceptance of love."*

~ Marianne Williamson

Have you noticed more love is being shown to you since you are showing more gratitude? How does this love feel to you? Are you comfortable with it, are you able to receive and return the love? If it makes you uncomfortable, look at the underlying feeling or doubt you may have? Write this down so you can be more aware and "unlearn the fear".

_____

_____

_____

_____

_____

_____

_____

_____

_____

_____

_____

_____

_____

November 6

Honoring my Beautiful Mother on Her Birthday

A trip to Teo in 2013 has opened my heart, and my life has been transformed. I have no words to describe what happened to me today. I took risks and jumped off cliffs I have only looked over before, and my lies of imperfection are so far gone. Who I thought I was has disintegrated into only the sweetness of the love in my heart. Life is great when I allow myself the gift to trust myself to shatter the lies I was fed from the dream of the planet and begin the journey into the light with me leading with my heart. I dearly love the sweetness reflected back to me in my teacher's eyes as I was willing to see myself clearly. I am grateful for love which has opened my eyes and my soul.

Laura Goodman The Shameless Warrior(tm) is the embodiment of reverent authentic love. Her mission is to lend her voice to Warriors of abuse who have not found theirs. Laura is an Author, Mentor, Warrior, Teacher, Speaker, and Advocate. She is here to serve humanity and loves with an open heart, fully and completely. Connect with Laura at www.facebook.com/pg/shamelesswarrior.

November 7

"Those who bring sunshine to the lives of others
cannot keep it from themselves."

~ James M. Barrie

How do you bring "sunshine" and gratitude to others? What are the feelings and thought you have when you do?

_____

_____

_____

_____

_____

_____

_____

_____

_____

_____

_____

_____

_____

_____

_____

_____

November 8

"The comfortable and comforting people are those who look upon the bright side of life; gathering its roses and sunshine and making the most that happens seem the best."

~ Dorothy Dix

Who or what type of person are you attracted to? What do you have in common with them? Are you now attracting people who are on the same journey as you? How does this support your journey?

_____

_____

_____

_____

_____

_____

_____

_____

_____

_____

_____

_____

_____

_____

_____

_____

_____

November 9

"The thankful receiver bears a plentiful harvest."

~ William Blake

How are you giving and receiving gratitude? To truly live a life of gratitude we learn to do both. Is there anything keeping you from receiving? Do you feel more comfortable giving? If so, why is it that? Once you know, then it is no longer hidden and can be overcome.

_____

_____

_____

_____

_____

_____

_____

_____

_____

_____

_____

_____

_____

November 10

> *"Gratitude is a fruit of great cultivation; you do not find it among gross people."*

~ *Samuel Johnson*

*(**Note:** Gross as in not yet learning or not being taught.).*

How are you cultivating and growing your gratitude? What are your daily habits, thoughts reminders to help you as you are on this journey?

_____

_____

_____

_____

_____

_____

_____

_____

_____

_____

_____

_____

_____

_____

November 11

I am so grateful for all the signs messages and synchronicity that I receive daily from God and the Angels that remind me and confirm to me I am right where I am so-post to be, and I am on the right path. When I find a feather, hear a special song on the radio or look at the clock and see that the time is 11:11 I know I am receiving Divine guidance.

I am so grateful that no matter what choices I make or through all the twists and turns of life there is a sacred presence that is always guiding me, loving me unconditionally and supporting me so I can fulfill my soul's purpose here on earth which Is Love! My life is a continuous stream of miracles grace and blessings, and I bow down in awe & reverence.

Prema Love is an Angel Guide, Sacred Musician, and Sound Alchemist/Sound Healer. Prema lives on Maui where she facilitates retreats, events and healing sessions to empower others to connect deeper to their true essence of Divine Love. "The medicine of the future will be music and sound" Edgar Cayce. Connect with Prema at www.premalovemusic.com.

November 12

"One kind word can warm three winter months."

~ Japanese proverb

How many months of winter are you warming? How often are you saying kind words? How often are we talking to ourselves or someone else and are we including a kind comment or remark? Are we appreciating, complimenting, thanking? For today or tomorrow, make it a point to say one kind comment to everyone you speak to, write about it on the next day.

_____

_____

_____

_____

_____

_____

_____

_____

_____

_____

_____

_____

_____

November 13

Today I am grateful for change in circumstances.

Ecclesiastes 3:1-8 There is a time for everything, and a season for every activity under heaven:
a time to be born and a time to die,
a time to plant and a time to uproot,
a time to kill and a time to heal,
a time to tear down and a time to build,
a time to weep and a time to laugh,
a time to mourn and a time to dance,
a time to scatter stones and to a time to gather them,
a time to embrace and a time to refrain,
a time to search and a time to give up,
a time to keep and a time to throw away,
a time to tear and a time to mend,
a time to be silent and a time to speak,
a time to love and a time to hate,
a time for war and a time for peace. (NIV)

What change in your life are you grateful for?

DeLyla Haunschild *is a Mother to two and a College Graduate. DeLyla's faith is the one constant that remains throughout her life; she knows she has so many blessings to be grateful and thankful to the Lord for experiencing. Follow DeLyla at www.facebook.com/DeLylaHaunschild or email at DeLyla.Global.247@gmail.com.*

_____

_____

_____

_____

_____

_____

_____

_____

November 14

Every day is truly a day of thanksgiving because His mercies are new each morning. Writing these words have opened my eyes to want to live more. As I look back over my life, I begin to think and when I begin to think I realize there's nobody like my God. He's brought from a mighty long way, and He's not through with me yet; that's a reason to praise and speak of my gratefulness. Where do you begin, when God has given you so many things to be grateful for. If I had ten thousand tongues, there still wouldn't be enough words to express how thankful, grateful and blessed I am. When you look at me you're looking at a miracle; you're looking at a sinner saved by grace, I don't look like anything I've been through; nobody did that but God. Rather up or down, good or bad, all things are working for me. From dangers seen and unseen, from my disobedience to my deepest hearts desires, God sees and knows all about me and loves me unconditionally and for that I am grateful. 1 Thessalonians 5:18 reads, "Give thanks in all circumstances; for this is the will of God in Christ Jesus for you."

Jada Andrews is a God-fearing mother, daughter, Disabled Veteran & small business owner, who's taken the challenges of life and turned them into stepping stones towards greatness. She is the owner of A Mustard Seed, she puts God first and walks in victory. Connect with Jada at www.facebook.com/AMustardSeed75.

November 15

In Dedication of Our Church Wedding, a change in my life as I turn towards God to guide my life and my marriage.

It had been my understanding that in marriage and life we must suffer and deal with it. Living depressed, although I had many reasons to be happy; feeling lonely and yet surrounded by people; unhappy and having everyone telling me how happy I should be; I had a feeling of emptiness I could not fill. My wonderful and very patient husband and I had been together for many years, one day we decided to have our union blessed with a church wedding. I prayed for God to change me and do as you want with me! That day I surrendered my doubts, my distrust, lack of confidence and unhappiness. I now know!! I have always been in His company and presence, not once have I been alone, I found happiness in Him and learned to love my self and His perfect creation.

"Joyful, joyful, we adore Thee, God of glory, Lord of love; hearts unfold like flowers before Thee, Opening to the Sun above, Melt the clouds of sin and sadness; drive the dark of doubt away; Giver of immortal gladness, fill us with the light of day!" ~ Van Dike

Claudia Nava *is a Wife and Mother of two children who loves to have fun and laugh!! She owns two businesses, Claudia Cleaning Services and a direct sales team with Stream. Connect with Claudia at* www.yoko4you.mystream.com

November 16

After 21 years of suffering, deprivation, and distress because physicians would not operate on me due to a difficult situation of fibroids in my abdomen, I finally got my life back via a physician who was willing to do God's work. On November 16, 2016, multiple of those demons were successfully removed, allowing me the chance and giving me the opportunity to move forward and live freely. Now, that I am in recovery, I am extremely thankful that my mind, body, and soul are safe. Always believe in yourself, stay persistent with perseverance until you reach your goal because God is able. Never give up because the universe is always on time to deliver. Embrace your journey and accept it for what it is, a gift to you. Accept your struggles, obstacles, and challenges as the path to cash into your blessings. Turn your deliverance into blessings because gratitude always comes within. Give praise, be grateful, by sharing your testimony touching lives of others. Allow yourself to be used for the highest good of others. Then, you will see that the journey was meant to be. Live in gratitude every day.

Martine M. Mayas was born in 1976 in New York to Haitian parents, Jocelyne Mayas and Frantz Mayas. Martine is a Natural Hair Enthusiast and an International Best Selling Author who shares her personal life experiences, style, poise, etiquette, class and sophistication with the world. Contact Martine at www.martinemayas.com.

November 17

We were anticipating my daughter giving birth to a beautiful baby girl. Now, this may seem like no big deal, babies are born every day. However, 12 years ago she lost a son who was born at 26 weeks and only made it eight days. She was broken and lost faith. I encouraged her to praise God for even little things every day. Four years later she was able to carry her now eight year old son to term after being on bed rest for most of the pregnancy. Between then and now she lost four more. As this pregnancy progressed, we praised God every single day for one more day of carrying our precious little one. She so wanted a daughter. We sang praises when told it was a girl. We would shout praises with every good report. We claimed the perfection of creation that is God. So on November 18th, via a scheduled C-section, our precious little Miracle was born. She will be a daily reminder that God renews the Spirit through Praises!

Vickie Washburn is a Teacher, Healer, Coach, and has been a Student of natural healing modalities, spirituality, and the root causes of the struggles we all face for the past 30 years. Connect with Vickie at www.vickiewashburn.com.

_____

_____

_____

_____

_____

_____

_____

_____

_____

_____

_____

November 18

Hezekiah Walker wrote a song entitled "Gratefulness" and it is a beautiful testimony of what my soul feels. "I am grateful for the things that you have done. Yes, I'm grateful for the victories we've one."

I realized no matter what man thought of me; God is the author of this story called life and nothing in this world matters but His thoughts towards me. Living in fear had to cease, "God has not given us the spirit of fear." Once you stop living by the world and start living by faith, you will see things in a light of God. I am blessed; no one did this but God.

My life has been a journey that God is not through with yet. I am more than a conqueror, more than an over-comer, more than a survivor, more than what this world says, God made me who I am, and in Him, I will live move and have my being. Grateful God sees the best in me, He knows my name, and He is the only one that has the final say. I am now on my quest to be who God has anointed me to be, and I will not stop until God is satisfied in my doing.

Jada Andrews is a God-fearing mother, daughter, Disabled Veteran & small business owner, who's taken the challenges of life and turned them into stepping stones towards greatness. She is the owner of A Mustard Seed, she puts God first and walks in victory. Connect with Jada at www.facebook.com/AMustardSeed75.

November 19

To me, gratitude is being grateful for the people and things in your life. It is also being appreciative of the life you were given. I am very grateful to have my mom and dad with me in my journey through life. They support me in all that I do, and I am very grateful for that. Expressing gratitude increases happiness in your life. When you express thanks and gratitude to someone, not only do you increase your appreciation for them, but you also boost that person's happiness level. If they knew that they helped you, they will feel valued in your relationship. If you are looking to create gratitude in your life, I would recommend reflecting on the people in your life and what they have done for you. I encourage you to write each person down on a list and tell them in person how much they helped you or how much they mean to you. Gratitude is simple to obtain. All you need is positivity, love, and honesty.

Olivia C. Witherspoon is currently a freshman in high school. Olivia loves to dance, play soccer, basketball, hike, read, and play her flute. Olivia's family is very important to her, and they are very close.

November 20

I have had a lifelong love affair with chocolate. Over the years our relationship became a dance of temptation, resistance, succumbing, and remorse…only to begin again.

Recently, I was given the honor of preparing a cacao ceremony for a New Moon celebration on Maui. As I worked with the raw cacao, imbuing it with my sacred intention to offer it in ceremony, I felt a vibration of aliveness coursing through my entire being. My deep devotion to chocolate had become a sacred expression. As I allowed myself to fully embrace this desire, I realized that it had always been calling to me, asking me to recognize its purpose in my life. Cacao ceremony is now an essential element of my life path, and I love to claim that my center is made of dark, rich, irresistible chocolate. How yummy is that?!!!

As I recognize and honor the sacred value of my deepest, darkest desires, I am overwhelmed by waves of gratitude for their presence and purpose in my life.

Gayle O Leary is a Gypsy Priestess, trusting the universe on her journey. She is on a quest to gather her tribe as she guides them to remember their Radiant Sacred Selves. Connect with Gayle at Gayle@GayleOLeary.com or Fb.me/RadiantPhoenixInternational

November 21

I am grateful for the moment when I received the Catholic planner. I did my research and noticed the "What are you grateful for?" section for every week and knew this was the planner for me. After I had received the planner, I began to create my daily plan to use.

These are the strategies that I use to have gratitude daily in my life:
First I plan for the week ahead to be prepared and be ready for the unexpected. I then write down as many things possible that I am grateful for that day, every day. There are days when I do forget and will make sure to write them down during the weekend.

Gratitude is defined as always being grateful for what you have, what you're going through and what you'll have in the future. Gratitude has helped me to be happy by knowing that life is precious and more than just the stuff in life.
My advice is to create gratitude is that you must always give it to others.

Ruby Kaluza is a Consultant with Thirty-One gifts, an Educator, Wife, Godmother, Sister, and Daughter. Born and raised in San Antonio TX, she is city lady with a country heart. Helping women fulfill their potential is what she loves to do. Connect with Ruby at www.facebook.com/SimplyRubyRed.

_____

_____

_____

_____

_____

_____

_____

_____

_____

_____

November 22

After having a healthy baby, I began suffering miscarriages. I was a Christian and teaching a women's Bible study, but I was not equipped for this attack. However, all that was about to change. God led me to John 10:10; the thief comes to kill, steal and destroy. Jesus came to give us life in abundance. In John 16:33; I learned that Jesus overcomes the world. These scriptures sustained and fueled me during this confusing time. I was hungry for His Word and His system of justice. Moreover, God, the Bible, and prayer became less random and more organized and logical. The Holy Spirit became alive in me. I began petitioning God using His scriptures similar to presenting a case in a Court of law.

I am thankful that God gave me life in abundance with two more healthy children. I'm thankful for a God that provides a book of promises to guide us down our daily path. Those promises *never* return void. Meditate on His Word daily to keep your mind aware of His *greatness.*

Sandy Moriarty *is a Wife and Mother of three kids. She has been a Licensed Attorney for over 20 years. As the Author of the book "My Logical Conclusion" and the blog mylogicalconclusion.com, God's Word is Sandy's logical conclusion for strength and empowerment. Women helping women achieve more is her mission.*

November 23

In Dedication to My Husband, Paul Ray.

I am grateful every day for you being in my life. After 18 years apart, we found each other, and we have now been married four years as I write this. You are my rock, steady, responsible, supportive and fun!! You are the one I am the closest to, who knows me best and knows what I need from you before I can even ask. I treasure our time together and how your consistent, meaningful attention and focus of me is like our anniversary every day. I do not need flowers or candy on Valentine's Day. You give me so much every day, I know I am special and loved every time I look at you, and every time you look at me. Gratitude is part of our life since I said "Yes" to being your wife. My heart and soul are filled with gratitude for the happiness and love we share as friends, business partners, and husband and wife.

Lisa Marie Ray is blessed to be an organ donor. She has five grown children and is married to her best friend. Lisa loves being a business owner, creating luscious chocolates at the Candy Wraptor, www.facebook.com/candywraptorliveshopping.

November 24

"One conscious breath is a meditation" ~ Eckhart Tolle

That gives you about 17,000 to 30,000 opportunities a day to meditate!

A conscious inhale is the most powerful and simplest act we can do to shift in the moment. It may be the only thing we have control over in that moment. The Breath is our life force energy, our spirit, chi, pranayama ....Do you ever take a moment out to acknowledge and give gratitude for such a simple yet powerful act? We do it so unconsciously but yet without we would seize to exist. Take a moment to breath in deeply and consciously. Take this very moment right now to send a thought of Gratitude to your breath. Let the breath breathe you, let it be your guide. Be witness to your breath. Where does it go in your body? What message does it have for you? Be in the flow with your breath and let it show you the power you have within you. So simple yet so powerful and always there for you!

Joy Brugh is a Life Transitions Coach, Shaman and Energy Healer specializing in empowering women through life's challenges and helping them to transform using a unique combination of modern life coaching, energetic and shamanic healing along with crystalline activations. Visit her at www.joybrugh.com or joy@joybrugh.com

November 25

"The man who radiates good cheer, who makes life happier wherever he meets it, is always a man of vision and faith."

~ Ella Wilcox

Who are you attracting in your life? Is it people who bring a smile, is cheery, is kind, and thankful? This is great, or do see people who are unhappy, complaining and not satisfied with anything? You do not need to stop seeing those people, be aware though of others affect us. When you are living in gratitude others who are living that way will want to be with you. A ripple effect of your gratitude can be anyone around you begins to be grateful.

Who have you attracted into your life lately? What are you learning from them?

_____

_____

_____

_____

_____

_____

_____

_____

_____

_____

_____

_____

November 26

God is. When the doctor said no, God said yes. Four premature gifts of God and I know God did it. I am so grateful God chose me to be the mother to four precious miracles. Though the road was rough watching them struggle for air to breath, and wondering what would life be like for them to try and catch up. God never makes a mistake, and he knew that they were going to be amazing. I learned what unconditional love felt like becoming their mother. When you die twice only to live and tell the story, nobody but God. A survivor of domestic violence, widow and single mother of four but I made it by God's grace. Grateful, oh yes I am; because it could've been me, it should've been me, it would've been me if it wasn't for grace and mercy. You've all heard the saying, "life is no crystal stair"? No matter what life gives, see the positive in it. Today's generation helped me with this because I have developed a life of #NoNegativeZone. Every day is a day of thanksgiving, wake each morning with a spirit of gratefulness, look yourself in the face and say, "I speak life, love, peace, prosperity and healing over my life." Put on the garment of positive and live the best you.

Jada Andrews is a God-fearing Mother, Daughter, Disabled Veteran & Business Owner, who's taken the challenges of life and turned them into stepping stones towards greatness. She is the owner of A Mustard Seed, she puts God first and walks in victory. Connect with Jada at www.facebook.com/AMustardSeed75.

November 27

Warrior Heart Revealed, Monique

I saw the truth of my soul bounce off of your eyes on top of Haleakala at sunrise as the fire of Pele ignited my heart. Sometimes it takes the clarity of another's heart, like a clean mirror, to reflect the reverence and vulnerability of our spirit to remind us of how sacred we are. I fell more in love with my own heart at that moment, witnessing the way the light passed through your spirit, as the soul recognized itself. I then witnessed my feminine spirit as it appeared in the first rays of the morning sun.

My gratitude was in the fact that there was recognition of the honor and integrity in one another. I embraced my heart that day on a deeper level, changing my life in an instant. My self-love appeared as a knowing that my heart will never forget. Sometimes the heart knows what the mind is incapable of comprehending. There are no words to describe these moments, as they are emblazoned deep within our hearts forever.

Laura Goodman The Shameless Warrior(tm) is the embodiment of reverent authentic love. Her mission is to lend her voice to Warriors of abuse who have not found theirs. Laura is an Author, Mentor, Warrior, Teacher, Speaker, and Advocate. She is here to serve humanity and loves with an open heart, fully and completely. Connect with Laura at www.facebook.com/pg/shamelesswarrior.

November 28

"Gratitude is the fountain from which all blessings
flow into your life."

~ Denise Joy Thompson

**What are the blessings flowing into your life since you are livening in gratitude?
Are they the blessings you thought you wanted in the past or are they blessings you
had never dreamt of or thought you would have?**

_____

_____

_____

_____

_____

_____

_____

_____

_____

_____

_____

_____

_____

_____

_____

November 29

*"To be able to practice five things everywhere under
heaven constitutes perfect virtue: gravity, generosity of soul, sincerity,
earnestness, and kindness."*

~ Confucius

**Which of these five are you practicing? What is the benefit to you from having
these in your life? How is having these in your life also benefitting others?**

_____

_____

_____

_____

_____

_____

_____

_____

_____

_____

_____

_____

_____

_____

November 30

In Honor of Everyone's Birthday

Today is my birthday. I wonder about life, why are we here, does our being here make sense? If I was God would I have created us the way we are? Did God know how we would evolve I and have we "evolved"? Sometimes we as a human race do not seem to have learned much over the many years that we have been around. Why war? Why famine, why epidemics which kill thousands of people? How do we contribute to all of those tragedies? We do not know the "bigger picture"?

All I know is I am here. I do not have control of anyone else, the most I can strive for is to be the person I can be; to be helpful and support others; to make a difference one life at a time. Every year I reflect on what I have done the previous year, I think I am doing pretty well, with reflection comes awareness and knowledge of how to do better. For now, I will concentrate on how to Live In Gratitude Daily and how this can change my life and the lives of those around me.

Denise Joy Thompson is a Wife, Mother of three furbabies, a #1 International Best-Seller Author, Coach, Colonel in the Air Force Reserve, a Therapist, and Veteran. She is the host of The Power Of A Woman's Voice TV show. Denise's mission is for everyone to create the life they can. Connect with Denise at thecoachalliance@gmail.com and www.facebook.com/LiveInGrattiudeDaily.

Thank you to Prema Love (11/11) for sharing the words of one her original songs.

I AM

I'm so inspired
I just have to sing
to count the blessings unfolding.
I'm so inspired
I just have to sing
to give thanks for the miracles I am beholding

I AM Healthy, I AM Abundant,
I AM Prosperous, I AM Triumphant
I AM great full, I AM Happy,
I AM Wealthy, & I love my life
I love this Life! I love My life
I love my Life! & I saver every drop of..

This Love, It's overflowing & it never runs dry,
for this Love is abounding, I see it in your lotus eyes.
 For this Love its ever flowing & it never runs dry, for this love is abounding.

I feel so much grace showering me
I feel the Beloved empowering me
to live my heart & souls passion completely.

I AM so great full I just have to dance.
I am intoxicated I am entranced,
with the holy spirit God Goddess Divine, Source, The beloved, its within that I find
My True Self

This Love, It's overflowing & it never runs dry,
for this Love is abounding, I see it in your lotus eyes.
For this Love its ever flowing & it never runs dry, for this love is abounding.

"A lifestyle of gratitude will reap limitless rewards."

~ Denise Joy Thompson

"Gratitude can warm our heart on a chilly day, chase away the clouds on a rainy day, and outshine the sun on a sunny day."

~ Denise Joy Thompson

December

December 1

"Gratitude is like a river, over time smoothing out the rough edges as it flows along its way."

~ Unknown

What are you noticing about yourself, in regards to the rough edges? Are you noticing you are not as reactionary? Do you notice you are calmer, less anxious and fearful? Are you smiling, laughing and joking more? Are you socializing more? What is different about you now, which you view as positive?

_____

_____

_____

_____

_____

_____

_____

_____

_____

_____

_____

_____

_____

_____

December 2

"Happiness cannot be traveled to, owned, earned, worn or consumed. Happiness is the spiritual experience of living every minute with love, grace and gratitude."

~ Denis Waitley

Now you know the route to happiness. How is your daily gratitude bringing you closer to the level of happiness you would like to have? Are you happy every day? Every hour? If not, do you know what is getting in the way? Once you know what is not helping or not working, then we can make changes for the better.

December 3

> *"Gratitude is the fairest blossom*
> *Which springs from the soul."*
>
> ~ *Henry Ward Beecher*

There are much growth and transformation which occurs when we live in gratitude.

What is the growth and transformation you see within yourself? Do you see more joy? Are you experiencing more emotions and empathy? What is different? What would you like more of?

_____

_____

_____

_____

_____

_____

_____

_____

_____

_____

_____

_____

_____

December 4

"Gratitude means to recognize the good in your life, be thankful for whatever you have, some people may not even have one of those things you consider precious to you (love, family, friends etc.). Each day give thanks for the gift of life. You are blessed."

~ Pablo

Without overthinking or analyzing, write down 15 people or things in your life you are grateful for, Ready, Set, Go!!

_____

_____

_____

_____

_____

_____

_____

_____

_____

_____

_____

_____

_____

_____

December 5

Today I am grateful for Godchildren. God's children. They are each made perfectly in His (the Lord's) eyes. Genesis 1:27 So God created man in His image, in the image of God he created him; male and female he created them. (NIV) Psalm 139:13-14 For you created my inmost being; you knit me together in my mother's womb. I praise you because I am fearfully and wonderfully made; your works are wonderful, I know that full well. (NIV) Children are an absolute blessing indeed.

Who are you truly grateful to the Lord for creating in your life?

DeLyla Haunschild is a Mother to two and a College Graduate. DeLyla's faith is the one constant that remains throughout her life; she knows she has so many blessings to be grateful and thankful to the Lord for experiencing. Follow DeLyla at www.facebook.com/DeLylaHaunschild or email at DeLyla.Global.247@gmail.com.

_____

_____

_____

_____

_____

_____

_____

_____

_____

_____

_____

_____

_____

December 6

"I think that real friendship always makes us feel such sweet gratitude, because the world almost always seems like a very hard desert, and the flowers that grow there seem to grow against such high odds."

~ Stephen King

We normally think of Stephen King and the suspense novels, such sweet words he shares about the gratitude of friendship.

Think of your friends, who and what about them are you grateful for?

_____

_____

_____

_____

_____

_____

_____

_____

_____

_____

_____

_____

_____

_____

December 7

"Gratitude is the ability to experience life as a gift. It liberates us from the prison of self-preoccupation."

~ John Ortberg

When we are grateful, we truly see the world around us; we are not limited to only seeing our self, or being self-absorbed. We are more aware and cognizant of everyone and everything around us. When we are in a state of gratitude, we see more ways and reasons to be grateful.

What have you noticed about yourself and your world since being on the Live In Gratitude Daily journey? How have you changed?

_____

_____

_____

_____

_____

_____

_____

_____

_____

_____

_____

_____

December 8

This year I am most grateful for the opportunity to reconnect with my adult children. My youngest, my son, was already living with us and 2 of my three daughters moved back home this year with their children. I was blessed to see all 3 of my grandchildren and my two daughters every day. I am filled with gratitude even for the stressful family times that tested our loyalty and love. I will be forever grateful for the times we shared filled with laughter, tears, and silence.

You have to know that everything is a choice, circumstances present themselves for a reason, and we can always choose to make lemonade.

I define gratitude as an opportunity to appreciate your daily circumstances. I know it helps me in going through life being happy because every day that you are grateful, you are also reminded that it could be different. My advice on how to stay in gratitude is to say one thing you are thankful for each day and when you see someone who is not grateful, show them the bright side and be grateful you are not in their ungrateful shoes.

Rhonda Holt is an Empowered Female, a Holistic Skin and Body Care Practitioner, a Business Owner, a Wife, Mother, and Grandmother. It is her passion to guide women on the path to discovering their feminine energy and be grateful for every step during the journey. Connect with Rhonda at www.rhondaholt.net.

December 9

"When you are grateful, fear disappears and abundance appears."

~ Anthony Robbins

Think about when you are fearful or anxious; how often is due to not having something, not having enough, wanting but not receiving? Often the idea of "lack" leads to fear. An antidote for fear is to be grateful for what we have, who we are, and what we can do. This does not mean if there is real danger (tigers, fire, attacker) that we do not remove ourselves from danger; it means to recognize fear is created. "Fear" is a story we have made up, danger is real which we need to protect ourselves from; fear is an emotion which we create, and we can "uncreate" it.

What are you "fearful" of? Now write down everything you are grateful for, your accomplishments, people who love you, and have in your life which can overpower, over-shadow, out-do your fear!! After writing everything you can think of, your fear will disappear!!

December 10

In dedication to my birthday

Be Yourself, Everyone Else Is Taken
~ Oscar Wilde

My favorite quote. I am grateful for everything which is me. This doesn't mean there is not work to do. It means I am who I am, for better or worse and I can make whatever changes are necessary to create the best me I can be. I am grateful for my life and being here. My birthday is a few days away, and I am going to be happy

Kim B. Smith *CEO of Bold Radio Station; Bold Authority Builder; # 1 International Best Selling Author, Radio Host. I enjoy yoga, walking, hiking, being out in nature and connecting with Mother Earth, being with friends and having great conversation with great wine and food! Connect at https://www.facebook.com/pg/KimBoudreauSmith.*

December 11

GRATEFUL LEADERSHIP AND LEADING WITH GRATITUDE

There are days when I find it can be difficult to align my heart and mind and be able to feel gratitude deeply. When this happens, I become what I now describe as 'frustratingly hopeful'; meaning – I know the feelings of angst and anxiety are temporary; but in the moment, I find the shift from 'hopeless to hopeful' sometimes takes longer than I'd like to accept.

And then, just as we never notice when our headaches disappear, we only notice when they are no longer hurting us – suddenly, one moment, you will realize you woke up on the other side of the heartache.

Sometimes this shift happens consciously; other times it requires effort. I've come to appreciate that when I have something significant to learn, the pain 'sticks around' long enough for me to notice it needs to be addressed.

I've realized that forgiveness, vulnerability, and generosity are a potent recipe to inspire one's heart back to openness.

I have come to be grateful for heartache. It reminds me what my heart aches for.

Miracles…

Laurie Vallas delights in observing the patterns between people and events and drawing unconventional associations between the two. She particularly enjoys the challenge of transforming these opportunities into meaningful, influential connections. The pursuit of revealing 'the heartifacts' within everything has become the foundation of Laurie's work. Happy to connect on FB: The Heartifacts, PositiviTEAs or at theheartifacts@gmail.com.

December 12

Dedicated to My One and Only, My Husband

I bless the day I met my husband. My life was about to take a turn for the better, and I did not even know it. In the last year of high school, with an uncertain future, no goals, no aspirations or hopes, my mother and I visited my brother's house; my mother and I drove three hours for what was my last Christmas vacation while in high school. The drive was uneventful, but as soon as we approached my brother's house we were behind a little old brown truck that was driven cautiously and attentive to traffic, which made my mom's road rage flourish. We followed this little truck all the way to my brother's home. Numerous blessings came to me from that day forward. **I met the young man that drove so cautiously, my now husband of 22 years.**

You are my destiny, you share my reverie, you are my happiness, That's what you are. You have my sweet caress, you share my loneliness, you are my dream come true that's what you are. ~ Anka, Paul. "You are my destiny".

Claudia Nava *is a Wife and Mother of two children who loves to have fun and laugh!! She owns two businesses, Claudia Cleaning Services and a direct sales team with Stream. Connect with Claudia at* www.yoko4you.mystream.com.

December 13

In Honor of My Mother and Father

"Gratitude unlocks the fullness of life. It turns what we have into enough, and more, it turns denial into acceptance, chaos to order, confusion to clarity. It can turn a meal into a feast, a house into a home, a stranger into a friend. Gratitude makes sense of our past, brings peace for today and creates vision for tomorrow. "
~Melody Beattie

I have had a rewarding, exciting life. I am grateful for the encouragement my mother gave me to dream bigger and expand my thinking to be worldwide, not just my familiar surroundings. I am grateful for my father showing me you can come from the poorest family and succeed with determination and hard work.

The most important message they both taught me was that you only have one name. It is important to do what you say you will and be respectful and kind to all. You must keep your honor so that when a handshake is all you are sealing a deal with, it rings as true as a notarized contract.

Saundra Lane is from Baton Rouge, LA and lives in Bandera TX. Saundra has a B.A. in Business and is the Owner of The Lane Agency since 1986 and tla2 Fashions, a women's clothing store. Connect with Saundra at www.facebook.com/saundralane

December 14

I am grateful to be an author with Cerebral Palsy. When you don't talk as well as you want to the best way to share your stories is in writing. In 2012, my best friend, Win Charles who also has Cerebral Palsy, wrote her biography to share her story to inspire people. I thought if she can do it, I can do it too.

It took me over two years to write my biography, If Dan Can Shred, You Can Too. It took me so long to write it because I typed so slow. As I was typing away, I learned that I have another voice inside of me that my family, friends, and myself had never heard before. It was amazing to me what I was typing. Every day that I was working on my biography, it was making me happier because I was going to inspire people with my story and they can hear my voice.

Once my biography was out, everyone loved my story, and it made me want to write more. If I can't tell my stories, I can share them in writing to inspire everyone.

Danielle Coulter, CEO/Owner of Dan Can Shred, is the first adaptive snowboarder in the world! She is a 5-time published author and an actor. Besides writing her bibliography, If Dan Can Shred So Can You, she also writes a children's series, The Adventures of Zoe. Connect with Danielle at http://www.dancanshred.com.

December 15

"What separates privilege from entitlement is gratitude."

~ Brené Brown

Do we "deserve" or are we "grateful for"? What is your perspective on life? At times it may be difficult to decide, do I deserve to be treated with respect or am I grateful to be treated with respect? Do I deserve a raise or am I grateful for a raise? Do I deserve a gift or am I grateful for a gift? We can remove ourselves from any situation which is not healthy or positive. We have many "privileges" which are not entitlements though they are often viewed as what we deserve, or it is our "right". I believe everything I have is because I have chosen it, good or bad, healthy or unhealthy, I chose it, and I can "unchoose" it. I am not saying this is easy; I can be grateful for everything in my life, whether it is a lesson or a gift. I am grateful for my journey, what I have in life, it has brought me to where I am today and can lead me to where I will be tomorrow.

What "privileges" are you grateful for in your life?

_____

_____

_____

_____

_____

_____

_____

_____

_____

_____

_____

December 16

"An attitude of gratitude brings great things."

~ Yogi Bhajan

Your attitude determines your altitude!! We can be flying high or laying low depending on our attitude. The lyrics from a popular song comes to mind, "Walking on sunshine" (are you now singing this with me?).

It only takes a moment to switch on the attitude of gratitude. Think of someone who makes you smile, see how quickly it can work? By simply thinking of someone or something which brings a smile to our face, we have a change in attitude, a change in our thinking, a change in our mindset. Now we can go throughout the day being grateful for the person or thing which makes us smile.

Who or what can you think of anytime you need an "attitude of gratitude"?

_____

_____

_____

_____

_____

_____

_____

_____

_____

_____

December 17

"Just an observation: it is impossible to be both grateful and depressed. Those with a grateful mindset tend to see the message in the mess. And even though life may knock them down, the grateful find reasons, if even small ones, to get up."

~ Steve Maraboli

For many people, the onset of winter and the holidays are not always as pleasant as we would like. It often becomes hectic and overwhelming, even when this is meant to be a joyous, loving and celebratory time of year. Take a moment and breathe, accept you are enough to bring joy to anyone and any occasion. This is about love and being with those we love and who love us.

Be grateful for all you have, be grateful for those you love, be grateful for being here. Write down what comes to mind as you think of who and what you are grateful for.

_____

_____

_____

_____

_____

_____

_____

_____

_____

_____

December 18

I am so grateful to have been born in a place and time where aging is not a barrier to living a rich and fulfilling life. As I approach my **65ᵗʰ birthday**, I remember the days when that age meant **retirement and slowly fading away**. My father, a member of the *Silent Generation*, never missed a day of work in his life. When he retired, he spent most of his days in a recliner watching TV and doing crossword puzzles.

That vision of work was never attractive to me. I have been blessed with a career as a law professor that makes a difference in the world. After more than twenty years teaching, I am ready to move on and do something more personally rewarding.

I am thankful that my generation of *Baby Boomers* has paved the way for the next stage of my life to be a period of **reinvention**. We are starting new businesses, writing books, and sharing our wisdom. I wake up every morning knowing that each day is a gift to be cherished.

Laurie Morin is a Law Professor, Activist, Entrepreneur, and Change-maker. She leads retreats where people reconnect with their passions and forgotten dreams, and design a plan to create more joy, meaning, and satisfaction in their lives. Connect with Laurie at www.lauriemorin.com.

December 19

"7 Effective Ways to Make Others Feel Important

1. Use their name.
2. Express sincere gratitude.
3. Do more listening than talking.
4. Talk more about them than about you.
5. Be authentically interested.
6. Be sincere in your praise.
7. Show you care."

~ Roy T. Bennett

In the hustle and bustle of the December holiday season, take a moment and show gratitude and appreciation for those in your life; family, friends, co-workers, anyone who contributes to your life. Growing up in a small town, we even gave a small gift to the mailman, the newspaper deliverer, anyone who provided us regular services and support.

Who is on your list to show gratitude and appreciation?

_____

_____

_____

_____

_____

_____

_____

_____

_____

December 20

"Gratitude is the single most important ingredient to living a successful and fulfilled life."
~ Jack Canfield

Remember Ebenezer Scrooge, (if not watch one of the original movies) due to a very sad circumstance in his life; he became ungrateful for everything and everyone. For him, it took "ghosts" to make him see what had been in his life all along and he became very grateful. Ebenezer became more successful and fulfilled when he gave away, with gratitude, his abundance. He became more abundant due to his new found gratitude.

What abundance have noticed or are more grateful for now than before you started to "live in gratitude daily?"

_____

_____

_____

_____

_____

_____

_____

_____

_____

_____

_____

_____

_____

December 21

On this date, my birthday, I realize how blessed I am with my life. Even though there have been bumps, potholes, and sharp curves, there has also been the most glorious travels and wonderful destinations. I am grateful for a multitude of things in my life, foremost my friends and family and my faith in God. God has given me the ability to come up with a solution even during the darkest times. God has given me a path along which He is beside me, along with my friends and family, helping and supporting me with my decisions. I am grateful I can see past difficult situations and come up with a plan B. There is saying "why stop at Plan B, there are 24 more letters of the alphabet." There is always a way to turn something around; I do not allow myself to stay stuck with a problem. I will find a way out with my faith and, as necessary, with the help of family and friends.

Amy Robinette is a Wife and Mother to a four-legged canine baby. Amy is a Multi-Business Owner and loves being her own boss! Amy spends many hours a week throughout Texas mentoring and supporting other women business owners. Connect with Amy at www.amyrobinette.com.

December 22

My Angel, Janis

The Holidays remind me that peace and love is our true nature. I am touched by the beauty of the spirit of the season. I am fond of the meaningful traditions that each family has put in place over the years that continue to touch our hearts with each passing year. True love can be defined as kindness and compassion. We all play a part in the global consciousness of good will towards all humanity.

I found Gratitude in my relationship with my own heart, as it directly affected how I treated my spouse and those closest to me. Once I became at peace within, then I was able to speak with kindness to those around me. This is what true love is about, supporting one another's dreams and being gentle and compassionate even in difficult times. We all need a safe place to land, and as adults, we can now begin to make healthier choices in the selection of a partner or spouse. May you find peace during the Holiday Season.

Laura Goodman The Shameless Warrior(tm) is the embodiment of reverent authentic love. Her mission is to lend her voice to Warriors of abuse who have not found theirs. Laura is an Author, Mentor, Warrior, Teacher, Speaker, and Advocate. She is here to serve humanity and loves with an open heart, fully and completely. Connect with Laura at www.facebook.com/pg/shamelesswarrior.

.

December 23

At a twenty-five-year high school reunion in Michigan, I learned that a classmate was terminally ill. I had many attendees sign a card, delivered it to his home and included my phone number. I was quite surprised to get a call. We shared a profoundly deep and honest conversation. About a year later, my friend passed. As I sat in prayer, I was moved to write:

"Bless the years it seems to take for change to come about
Take yet another breath and blow the candles out
In gratitude for each moment spent here on earth, heaven sent.
Sometimes we circle round, heaven bound."

I'm profoundly grateful I took the action to reach out. I was reminded we often get caught up in berating ourselves for not attaining our goals and dreams or not keeping our promises to break a bad habit. We put conditions on appreciating our lives and forget the immense gift just being alive is. Any day is the perfect day to be grateful you were born.

Bentley Kalaway is a Singer/Songwriter, Author and Coach and an Evolutionary Beacon for the Emergence of the Empowered Embodied Feminine. She is passionate about supporting others to claim, amplify and act upon their inner wisdom for their own fulfillment and our collective evolution. www.facebook.com/BentleyKalawayMusic

December 24

When I think of the word gratitude, I think of how important it is to let go of negative experiences and replace the experience with something positive learned from that experience. Did you know that negative responses derive from negative perceptions? Why must the negative experience be held on to when it's many things to appreciate more, instead? Many times there's comfort complaining as if complaining changes things, but it only validates why you're upset. The reasons you are upset do not have to be validated. The validation of why you chose to be upset starts with you. You control those triggers, but instead, complaints are put out in the universe when instead it could be used to create a more controlled path to a healthier lifestyle. We have to be kind to our mind and make room for thoughts that will help us to grow. One should identify the issue and write it down to remove it from the mental psyche. Once the negative experience is written down, identify with what you learned about yourself using only positive thoughts. Positive thoughts are linked to a healthier body and clearer mind, while negative thoughts induce stress. And too much stress can harm our bodies. So by creating a daily journal of what you're grateful for will shift your mind into focusing on things you enjoy, things that bring you happiness, and things that excite you daily.

Candice Merritt is CEO of Peaceful Solutions in San Antonio, TX. Candice shares her passion for serving others by providing mediation services as an alternative to court. Peaceful Solutions offers mediation services, motivational speaking engagements, and conflict resolution workshops. Follow Candice at www.facebook.com/Peacefulsolutionsmediation.

December 25

I often find myself looking ahead to more fulfilling and rewarding projects instead of finishing what has been placed before me for that day. I want to get to the good stuff. Looking ahead invites impatience, and a restlessness washes over me in areas where I'm not focused on giving my best at that moment. In essence, I'm saying that my task, at hand, is less important than what I'm looking ahead to tomorrow or next week. In my daily grind of laundry, preparing meals and running a business I often feel ungrateful. Maybe because it lacks instant gratification. But, what I have come to understand in 25 years of marriage and motherhood is that giving my best to what God has placed before me at that very moment is being grateful and it whispers, "It is enough." God can take my seemingly insignificant act, multiply it, and create abundance in my life. Thankfulness prepares my heart to enrich another person's life and help them flourish in ways I can never imagine.

Jackie Liberto is happily married to Dan for 25 years and the parents of three daughters. Jackie is a travel and lifestyle blogger at Jackieliberto.com where she writes about family and travel and how you can have fun at both. www.Facebook.com/thefreedomgirls

December 26

"Christmas gives us the opportunity to pause and reflect on the important things around us - a time when we can look back on the year that has passed and prepare for the year ahead."

~ David Cameron

December is a month of many holidays and special occasions. There is a simple message in everything we celebrate during this time of year: be grateful, be kind, be love.

Take a moment, a quiet moment today, to reflect on all you are grateful for. What is the feeling or thought that comes to mind? Write this down and carry it in your heart through the New Year.

_____

_____

_____

_____

_____

_____

_____

_____

_____

_____

_____

_____

December 27

Dedicated to My Daughter, Laura

We have the blessing of living in a country where women have choice and opportunity not afforded to women in much of the rest of the world. I am grateful that my daughter had the same right to education as my son. I am grateful that my daughter knows that she is enough as she is and that she does not have to be a wife or a mother to have value. I am grateful that my daughter speaks her mind and her truth and is willing to walk away from a situation that is not in her highest, best interest.

I am grateful that my daughter made choices in her life that have kept her choices open to her. (Excerpt from my letter in the book "Dear Amazing Daughter".)

Gayle O Leary is a Gypsy Priestess, trusting the universe on her journey. She is on a quest to gather her tribe as she guides them to remember their Radiant Sacred Selves. Connect with Gayle at Gayle@GayleOLeary.com *or Fb.me/RadiantPhoenixInternational*

December 28

Two Hearts Became One Forever

Being supported by angels, my protector Miguel stands tall on the hill at the Basilica of our Lady of Guadalupe in Mexico City. He heard your cries from around the world and together with Le Virgincita and almighty God, this humbled Warrior's heart is beyond speechless. Humility is an understatement.

I am in gratitude for each day, and each breath I take. There are no words for the depth of love I feel for everyone in my life. I bow to each of you and please keep the prayers coming for acceptance, peace, and love. One Love Connects Us All. I am living in gratitude today and always.

Laura Goodman *The Shameless Warrior(tm) is the embodiment of reverent authentic love. Her mission is to lend her voice to Warriors of abuse who have not found theirs. Laura is an Author, Mentor, Warrior, Teacher, Speaker, and Advocate. She is here to serve humanity and loves with an open heart, fully and completely. Connect with Laura at* www.facebook.com/pg/shamelesswarrior.

December 29

In Memory of Frank M.

To me, the word success has been hijacked and mangled. God personally gave me a new definition of success. Success can never be found in a number on a scale, a new purse or house lived in. It can't be driven or achieved because of the number in your bank account. Success for me is in my heart and my relationship with God. It's the confidence I have for being uniquely and lovingly me. Talk about gratitude...

Chasing things creates more chasing and never-ending comparing ourselves to others. When we allow God to fill that empty longing in our hearts, we become confident in who we are. Then when we lose weight, it's for the right reason. Then when we enjoy a nice vacation, car, home, jewelry or anything else, it is a blessing and a gratitude. Why? Because we are not expecting those "things" to fill something missing. If you can't find gratitude in being you and are still searching for your emptiness to be filled by outside things you will never feel successful within you. Start a gratitude journal and watch your life and your confidence change.

Sandy Lee-- Sandy means helper and Lee means healer. It is Sandy's life mission to use her gifts, her purpose and the struggles she has overcome to help you overcome yours. Finding your God-given Confidence IS Success and discovering this is transformational and teaches you to finally fly. Find Sandy at happy@sandyleecoaching.com.

December 30

"As the year comes to a close, it is a time for reflection – a time to release old thoughts and beliefs and forgive old hurts. Whatever has happened in the past year, the New Year brings fresh beginnings. Exciting new experiences and relationships await. Let us be thankful for the blessings of the past and the promise of the future."

~ Peggy Toney Horton

The end of the year is a great time to reflect on the blessings of the past year. You are here, reading this. Be grateful for the days that are past and the present you are living now.

Irene Pro is CEO of ICK Communication llc, which includes ICK Publishing, We Are Beautiful Magazine©, and We Are Beautiful Teens©. Irene lives in New Jersey with her husband, three beautiful children, three dogs, three cats, and four chickens!!

www.wearebeautifulmagazine.com

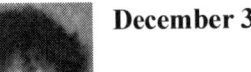

December 31

The last day of the year, and the last day of my Air Force career in 2011. As I got ready for the next chapter in my life, I reflected on the previous 26 years. I was grateful for the many supervisors who also were my mentors. I could see in hindsight how I was a combination of their cumulative influence. TSgt Bostic taught me how to separate personal and professional situations. MSgt Eckberg helped me determine whether I should reenlist or separate after my first enlistment. MSgt Harris taught me how to research information before challenging a process. He didn't answer my questions; he showed me how to find the answers.

All these influences are still a huge part of my life. These skills span all aspects of my life, and I am grateful to have had the ability to listen to my gut feeling in joining the Air Force. It was a great influence in my life, and all my experiences have brought me here, to who I am today.

Kimberly Meyers *served 26 years in the Air Force; upon retiring she created her fitness business, Fitness Kinektions. She has 24 years' experience as a group fitness instructor, is a certified Leadership Coach, personal trainer and holds an Associates in Kinesiology. Connect with Kimberly at* www.fitnesskinektions.com

For the rest of the journey.......

If you started this journal on January 1, you have come to the end only of this initial part of a lifelong journey of Gratitude. If you are reading this and not quite finished with the entire 365 days, we will see you here on your 366th day.

This year is only the beginning of your **Live In Gratitude Daily** life's journey.

The co-authors and I hope you will continue with us each year, learning and growing with us.

As you end one year, 365 days of gratitude, what would you like to see in yourself as you start the next 365 days? Write down the growth and personal changes now and after your next 365 days, see how much more you gained that what you are thinking of right now.

Blessings for a great life as you **Live In Gratitude Daily**.

Denise Joy Thompson

My growth and transformation for the next year includes:

_____

_____

_____

_____

_____

_____

_____

_____

_____

INDEX

Last	First	Date
Lee	Sandy	7/7, 7/17, 12/29
Leyva-Hill	Jacqi	8/8
Liberto	Jackie	12/25
Love	Prema	11/11
Marco	Jeanette B	6/14, 9/30
Mayas	Martine A	11/16
Merritt	Candice	12/24
Meyers	Kimberly	7/14, 11/19, 12/31
Moore	Laurie Hartley	1/4, 8/11
Moore	Shavannah	5/3
Moriarty	Sandy	1/20, 11/22
Morin	Laurie	10/10, 12/18
Nava	Claudia	4/30, 5/30, 11/15, 11/12
Parks	Dr. Joyce A.	1/3
Offutt	Crystal	5/27
Offutt	Lisa Renee	9/9
O Leary	Gayle	10/27, 11/20, 12/27
Shade	Colleen	10/17
Parmar	Mansi	1/6, 3/6, 8/5
Pineda	Alma Soul	2/13, 7/24, 8/27, 10/1
Prokopiw	Alexandria	2/23
Prokopiw	Irene	1/2, 12/30
Prokopiw	Michael	5/26
Prokopiw	Theodora I.	3/14
Ray	Lisa Marie	11/23
Riordan, Ph.D.	Minette	1/13, 4/27
Robinette	Amy	12/21
Schroeder	Judith Richardson	4/11, 9/21
Smith	Kim B.	12/10
Solis	Angelica	10/20
Sparks	Chanette	6/1
Stein, Ph.D.	Cara	7/22
Stokes	Marlene Grimes	5/2
Stout, Ph.D.	Wendy	7/21, 8/30
Sumner	Brittany L	1/21, 3/17, 11/4
Taylor	Geraldine	6/6, 7/18, 9/25
Thomas	Karen A.	3/10
Thompson	Denise Joy	1/16, 4/14, 7/1, 10/2, 10/19, 11/30
Trumet	Sharlene	5/22, 9/6
Vallas	Laurie	3/12, 4/1, 7/11, 12/11
Wade	Holly	5/13
Washburn	Vickie	9/10
Wharmby	Mary Scheske	1/25
Witherspoon	Caroline	7/12
Witherspoon	Olivia	11/19
Wiszowaty	Janet	7/15, 9/11

Made in the USA
Charleston, SC
11 February 2017